How to
LEARN
CHINESE

WITHOUT EVEN TRYING!

First published in the United Kingdom in 2018 by
Batsford
43 Great Ormond Street
London WC1N 3HZ
An imprint of Pavilion Books Company Ltd

ISBN: 9781849944557

A CIP catalogue record for this book is available
from the British Library.

10 9 8 7 6 5 4 3 2 1

Reproduction by Mission, Hong Kong
Printed by Toppan Leefung Printing Ltd, China

This book can be ordered direct from the publisher
at the website www.pavilionbooks.com, or try your
local bookshop.

How to
LEARN
CHINESE

WITHOUT EVEN TRYING!

FREYA YANG

BATSFORD

Table of Contents

zài jiā

在家

At Home
This chapter covers different areas of the home and how to describe locations.

miáo shù

描述

Describing Things
Here we will learn how to describe things, including weather conditions.

Glossary
Answers

huó dòng

活动

Activities
The subject of this chapter is actions and activities.

shēng huó

生活

Work and Study
In this final chapter, we'll look at the subjects of studying and jobs.

How to Learn Chinese

* Descriptive

Descriptive words are not essential in all sentences, but in some cases they can add extra information. Their place in the sentence is flexible depending on the subject matter.

example:

hǎo

好

good

1. Noun

The main subject is usually at the beginning of the sentence. It is usually a person, but it could also be an object, an event or something else. Their function is to lead a Chinese sentence.

example:

mā   ma

妈妈

mum

2. Time

As verbs in the Chinese language have no conjugation, it is very important to use time words to state when an action took place. These usually come immediately after the subject. It is important not to put them at the end of the sentence (where they frequently appear in English).

example:

jīn   tiān

今天

today

*Question

Forming a question in Chinese is more straightforward than forming a question in English. Just replace the relevant part of the sentence with the appropriate question word.

example:

zài nǎ

在哪

where?

* Modifier

Modifiers are words we add either to modify the meaning of a sentence (such as 不 that makes a sentence negative) or to connect elements of a sentence together. The place of modifiers in a sentence is also flexible.

example:

bù

不

not

3. Place

If you want to specify where something happened (e.g. at school, in Beijing), you will often use a phrase beginning with 在. This phrase needs to come after the time word, but before the action.

example:

zài jiā

在家

at home

4. Action

Unlike Western languages, in Chinese an action usually appears at the end of the sentence. This is mainly because we do not have tenses, so it is very important to state other conditions such as time and place before stating the action.

example:

chī fàn

吃饭

eat

Pinyin Tones

Chinese is a melodic and tonal language, and tones are one of the first things to tackle when learning Chinese. These tones are called 四声, four tones, however there is also a fifth one called 轻声, neutral tone. It is very important to associate the correct tone with the right character, because incorrect tones could mean other characters that have completely different meanings (as demonstrated below). Therefore, it is imperative to learn the correct pronunciation to avoid any unwanted misunderstandings.

flat tone

going up

1. First tone

The first tone is flat and straight. Its monotone quality makes it almost like a high musical note. The important thing about this tone is to not change the note when speaking.

mother

2. Second tone

The second tone is the rising tone. This tone usually starts from a lower pitch but ends at a slightly higher pitch. It sounds like someone asking a question ('Huh?')

sesame

Chinese is a tonal language. Even for the same syllable, there can be various pronunciations.

down and up

going down

light

3. Third tone

The third tone goes down and rises again. However, in conversation, it could be very fast, so the most characteristic thing people notice is that it is low.

4. Fourth Tone

The fourth tone is the falling tone. It needs to start at a slightly higher pitch than all the other tones, and then go quickly downwards. Sometimes people think this tone sounds angry.

5. Neutral tone

The fifth tone is the neutral tone, or the soft tone as the Chinese call it. It has no emphasis, and usually comes and goes fast. It is given very little stress compared to other tones.

horse

scold

question

Pinyin Initials

Pinyin is a rather recent invention. It was developed in the 1950s by Chinese linguists in an attempt to use the Roman alphabet to indicate the pronunciation of Chinese characters.

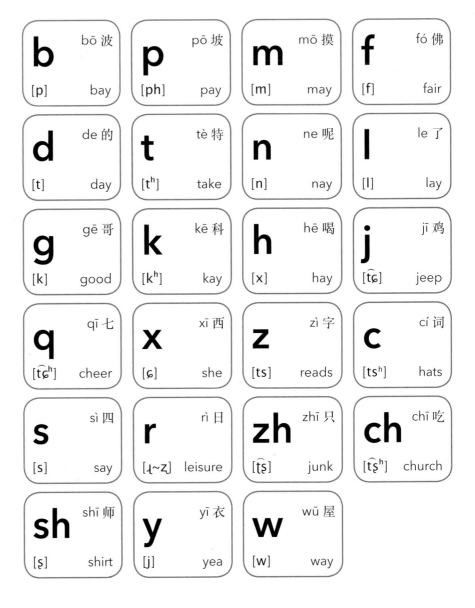

b bō 波 [p] bay	**p** pō 坡 [pʰ] pay	**m** mō 摸 [m] may	**f** fó 佛 [f] fair
d de 的 [t] day	**t** tè 特 [tʰ] take	**n** ne 呢 [n] nay	**l** le 了 [l] lay
g gē 哥 [k] good	**k** kē 科 [kʰ] kay	**h** hē 喝 [x] hay	**j** jī 鸡 [tɕ] jeep
q qī 七 [tɕʰ] cheer	**x** xī 西 [ɕ] she	**z** zì 字 [ts] reads	**c** cí 词 [tsʰ] hats
s sì 四 [s] say	**r** rì 日 [ɻ~ʐ] leisure	**zh** zhī 只 [tʂ] junk	**ch** chī 吃 [tʂʰ] church
sh shī 师 [ʂ] shirt	**y** yī 衣 [j] yea	**w** wū 屋 [w] way	

Pinyin Finals

Most of the sounds in Chinese can be written in 声母 (consonant) + 韵母 (vowel). Sometimes just 韵母 (vowel). But it is necessary to point out that Pinyin is not Chinese. It is merely a pronunciation guide for Chinese characters that are used in daily communication.

yùn
韵
mǔ
母
biǎo
表

a ā 阿 [a] father	**o** wō 窝 [o] saw	**e** é 鹅 [ɤ] her	**i** yī 一 [i] see
u wū 屋 [u] rude	**ü** yú 鱼 [y] French *tu*	**ai** ài 爱 [ai] eye	**ei** bèi 被 [ei] bay
ui shuǐ 水 [uei] wait	**ao** ǎo 袄 [au] now	**ou** ōu 欧 [ou] oh	**iu** liú 流 [iou] yoke
ie yé 爷 [iɛ] yes	**üe** yuè 月 [yɛ] ü+eh	**er** ér 儿 [ə] are	**an** ān 安 [an] can
en ēn 恩 [ən] turn	**in** yīn 音 [in] in	**un** chūn 春 [uən] went	**ün** yún 云 [yn] German *grün*
ang fáng 房 [aŋ] German *gang*	**eng** dēng 灯 [əŋ] sung	**ing** yīng 应 [iŋ] sing	**ong** dōng 冬 [uŋ] German *lunge*

Character Stroke Orders

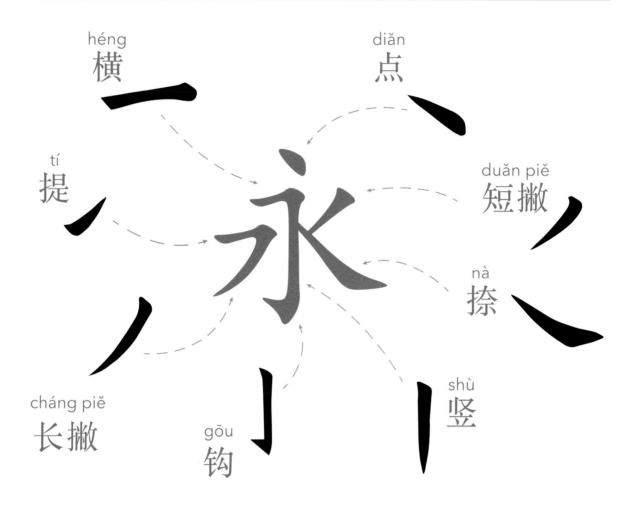

The Eight Principles of Yong 永字八法

Chinese characters are the most widely used and also the oldest continuously used system of writing in the world. They are logograms that have evolved over thousands of years from oracle bone script (texts inscribed on animal bones or turtle shells first used in the 2nd century BCE). Over time, the shapes and meanings of characters have changed hugely as the language has become unified. Characters are constructed by radicals (a graphical component of the character) and these radicals are contructed by certain common strokes (as 永字八法 shown above). The Chinese also developed rules of stroke order to help people remember how the character is best written.

1. Horizontal before vertical

When horizontal and vertical strokes cross, the horizontal stroke is usually written before the vertical stroke.

一　十

2. Diagonals right-to-left before left-to-right

For characters with symmetrical diagonals, right-to-left diagonals (ノ) are written before left-to-right diagonals.

ノ　人

3. From top to bottom

As a general rule, strokes are written from top to bottom, especially for characters that have stacked-up structures.

一　二　亐

4. From left to right

Some characters with radicals have a left-right structure. They are also written from left to right.

了　子　孔

5. Enclosure before content

For characters with an enclosure, the frame needs to be created first before it is filled with content.

ノ　几　月　月

6. Close frame last

Bottom strokes for enclosures are written last. A common saying is 'Put people inside, then close the door.'

丨　冂　日　日

7. Centre before outside

For vertically symmetrical characters, the centre part is written before components on the left and right.

亅　小　小

Chinese Measure Words

'a glass of water'

Measure words are used together with numbers and nouns to indicate the quantity of an object. In this case, the concept in English is rather similar. Water here is measured in glasses. So we say 一杯水 (one glass of water).

'a person'

The concept here is more abstract. In this situation we need to quantify 人 (people) as well, and we use the character 个 as a measure word. So we say 一个人, as in English 'one person'. Note that the measure word 个 here is not translated as it is a concept absent in English.

The Chinese have measure words for all the objects in the world. How should we employ these measure words?

gè	suì	běn	xiē	kuài
个	岁	本	些	块
general	age	publications	some	money

For example:

   'a father'

yī 一 gè 个 bà ba 爸爸

   'eight years old'

bā 八 suì 岁

    'three books'

sān 三 běn 本 shū 书

    'some apples'

yī 一 xiē 些 píng guǒ 苹果

shí 十 kuài 块 qián 钱 'ten yuan (money)'

rén

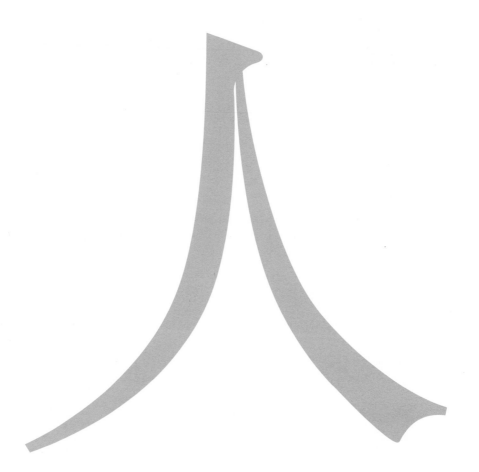

People

In this chapter we will learn how to refer to oneself and to others. We will start by introducing Chinese personal pronouns and learn how to modify them into possessive pronouns by adding one simple character. After that, we will present a couple of useful verbs, and learn how to create negative sentences. We will then move on to introduce pronouns, such as 'this', 'that' and 'which', as well as vocabulary pertaining to people. By the end of this chapter we will be able to construct basic Chinese sentences and refer to various family members and daily objects.

Building Blocks

de

的

possession

的 is a modifier that can be placed after any personal pronoun to form a possessive personal pronoun.

e.g. 你的、他们的

people

rén
人

人 is the character for people in Chinese. It is easily recognizable as it looks like a person walking.

I

wǒ
我

he

tā
他

you

nǐ
你

we

wǒ men
我们

they

you

nǐ men
你们

tā men
他们

to be

是 means 'to be'. However, it is employed slightly differently in Chinese: 是 cannot be used when describing objects using adjectives. For instance, when in English we would say 'he is tall', in Chinese we simply say 他高 (he tall); 是 is used when employing nouns, as in 'he is a person': 他是人 (he is person).

e.g. 我是、他们是、你们是

to have, there is

The original meaning of 有 is 'to exist', however it has changed slightly over time and can currently be likened to the English phrases 'to have' and 'there is/are'. When used in conjunction with people it means 'to have' as in 我有 (I have ...). When it doesn't involve people, it means 'there is'.

e.g. 我们有、你有

not

The character 不 is placed before a verb/adjective/adverb to create a negative sentence. The only exception to this is 有 (to have).

e.g. 你不是、他们不是

not (have)

没 is placed in front of 有 (to have) to create 没有 (don't have). This works both as a verb and an auxiliary. Note that 有 works with 没 but not 不.

e.g. 他没有、我没有

Father
爸爸 means 'father'. It is a combination of 巴 (ba) which indicates the sound, and 父 which means paternal, axes and labour.
e.g. 我爸爸、你爸爸

Mother
妈妈 means 'mother'. It is a combination of 马 (ma), which indicates the sound, and 女 which is the radical for 'female'.
e.g. 他妈妈、你妈妈

Son
儿子 means 'son' or 'boy'. 儿 has the meaning of 'offspring' and 子 indicates that it is a masculine offspring.
e.g. 爸爸的儿子、我的儿子

Daughter
女儿 means 'daughter' or 'girl'. 女 is the radical for 'female' and 儿, just like in 儿子, means offspring.

e.g. 妈妈的女儿、她的女儿

Sir
先生 was originally used to address someone older or wiser. It has evolved into the equivalent of 'Sir' or 'Mister'.
e.g. 这个先生、先生的女儿

Miss
小姐 is used to address an unmarried woman, similar to 'Miss' in English. 小 means 'little', and 姐 means 'sister'.
e.g. 那个小姐、小姐的儿子

this

这 means 'this', as in referring to something in close proximity. However when paired with 儿 (er) or 里 (li) it means 'here' as in 'this place'. 这儿 is commonly used in the north of China, whereas southerners prefer to use 这里.
e.g. 这个先生、这个小姐、这儿

that

那 can be translated as 'that,' as in referring to something which isn't in close proximity. Just like 这, it can be paired with 儿 or 里 to give 那儿 or 那里, meaning 'that place' or 'over there'. Once again, northerners favour 那儿, whereas southerners prefer 那里.
e.g. 那是、那个人、那个爸爸、那儿

who?

谁 is a question word similar to 'who' in English. It can be pronounced 'shei' or 'shui'. The latter is more formal.

e.g. 是谁、谁的

which

哪 is a question word that can be translated to 'which'. It can also be paired with 儿 and 里, giving 哪儿 or 哪里, which means 'where' (which place). 哪儿 is more habitually employed in the north of China, whereas 哪里 is commonly heard in the south.
e.g. 哪个人、哪儿 、哪里

Exploring the Language

Let's have a look at the simplest form of a sentence in Chinese: subject + action. The subject could be anything, from people and personal pronouns, to objects and many other things. The subject usually appears at the beginning of the sentence. The action usually contains a verb. If we want to specify the object that the action is applied to, we could also include the object as part of the action. Also note that when we want to make a negative sentence, negative modifiers are placed immediately before the action.

Something is/has something.

For example:

This is father.   This is my father.

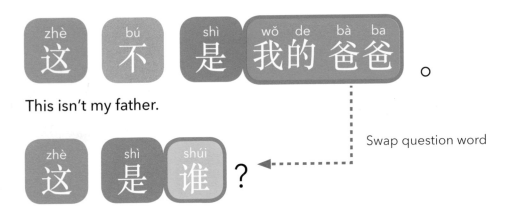

This isn't my father.

Swap question word

Who is this?

Can you translate these conversations? See page 128 for the answers.

zhè shì shúi
这 是 谁 ？

Xiangmao

zhè shì wǒ de bà ba
这 是 我 的 爸爸 。

Longlong

nà shì shúi
那 是 谁 ？

nà shì wǒ de mā ma
那 是 我 的 妈妈 。

Longlong & Xiongmao in China

wáng xiān shēng yǒu ér zi ma
王 先 生 有 儿 子 吗 ？

méi yǒu wáng xiān shēng yǒu nǚ ér
没 有 ，王 先 生 有 女 儿 。

nǎ ge shì tā de nǚ ér
哪 个 是 他 的 女 儿 ？

nà ge shì tā de nǚ ér
那 个 是 他 的 女 儿 。

Practice Time

Using what we have learned in this chapter as a guide, try and match these character building blocks with their appropriate meaning.

Time to test your vocabulary knowledge! Try to pay attention to the characters as well as their Pinyin.

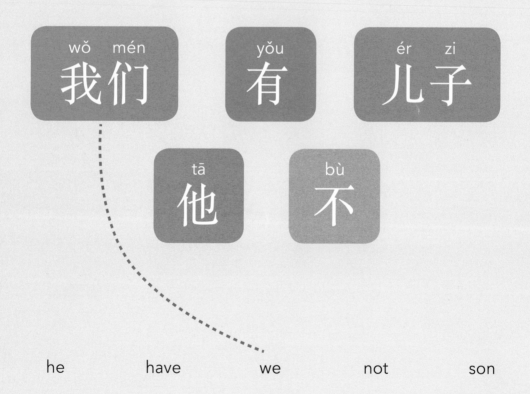

Basic Characters

people

The original oracle bone script pictogram of this character was meant to look like a side view of a standing primate, with a hunched back and arms hanging down loosely. It was intended to symbolize work and craftsmanship as well as the early manufacturing of tools.

Evolution of pictographic characters:

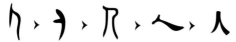

不

not

This character was originally a pictogram of an early handheld weapon used in ancient China. It was made by sharpening bamboo into three deadly prongs, similar to the Western trident. It has evolved into expressing the negative because of its link with danger and death.

Evolution of pictographic characters:

Fifty-six Chinese Ethnicities

zhōng
中

huá
华

mín
民

zú
族

During its long and rich history, many different peoples and tribes of various origins and creeds have settled in China. According to a government census, there are 56 ethnicities 民族 (ethnicities) spread across the country. Among these, the most predominant ethnicity is called 汉 (Han), which makes up 91.51 per cent of the country's total population. The remaining 8.49 per cent are referred to as 少数民族 (minor ethnicities) by the Chinese government. Among these, the largest is called 壮族 (Zhuang Zu), with a population of 18 million, and the smallest is called 珞巴族 (Luo Ba Zu), with a population of less than 3,000. People of minor ethnicity can be found throughout the country. Many of them frequently interact with Han society as well as preserving and upholding their own culture and values.

The Han stands at a population of 1.24 billion, and can be found in every province in China. They more commonly reside in the middle and lower reaches of the Yellow River, the Yangtze River and the Pearl River. They can also be found well represented in the north-eastern part of the country. It is the longest surviving ethnicity in the world, having existed for over 4,000 years. On top of that, the Han comprise the largest ethnic group in the world, at 19 per cent of the planet's total population. Over the course of history, the Han have excelled at agriculture and craftsmanship. Education has always been very important to the Han, and the teachings of philosophers, such as Confucius and Mencius, have greatly affected Han values and way of life.

Although they make up a small percentage of the country's total population, the 55 minor ethnicities can be found all over China. The regions they more commonly reside in are the south-west, north-west and north-east. The Yun Nan province in the south-west is currently home to 25 minor ethnic groups, more than any other province. To promote equality between ethnic groups, the government has introduced policies to ensure that peace and respect for people's faiths and customs are upheld. These policies have led to the establishment of five autonomous regions: Inner Mongolia, Xin Jiang, Guang Xi, Ning Xia and Xi Zang (Tibet). This helps people from minor ethnicities to promote their culture and take part in local government decisions.

There are 56 ethnicities in China! It is a big melting pot with all kinds of people from different cultures.

Minor Chinese Ethnicities

壮族
Zhuang Zu

With a population of over 18 million, Zhuang Zu is the largest minor ethnic group in China. Although in recent years some of them have converted to Christianity, many still practise their native religion, which centres on praying to their ancestors and to a wide pantheon.

回族
Hui Zu

Another fairly large minor ethnic group in China is the Hui Zu people, with a population of around 10 million. The Hui Zu can be traced back to the 13th century, when many Islamic people immigrated from Central Asian countries. Although they have cohabited alongside the Han for centuries, many of the Hui Zu still practise Islam.

维吾尔族
Wei Wu'er Zu

The word Wei Wu'er comes from the Turkic Uygur, which means 'unity' or 'people coming together'. Their ancestors were nomadic Turkic pastoralists known as 'Tiele'. The Wei Wu'er Zu speak their own language, which has evolved from a branch of Turkic and is written using the Persian alphabet. They are famous for their agriculture, and are the largest producers of grapes in China.

shí

时

jiān

间

Talking Time

This chapter is all about indicating and asking for the time. We'll start by learning about the Chinese numerical system and how to count up to 99. We'll also learn the way that the Chinese count on their fingers, which can come in handy. This will be followed by vocabulary regarding different periods of time such as 'week', 'month' or 'year'. We will also learn how to tell the time of day and enquire about it. As there is no conjugation in Chinese, it is very important to learn how to state time appropriately. This should be very easy to do by the end of this chapter.

Building Blocks

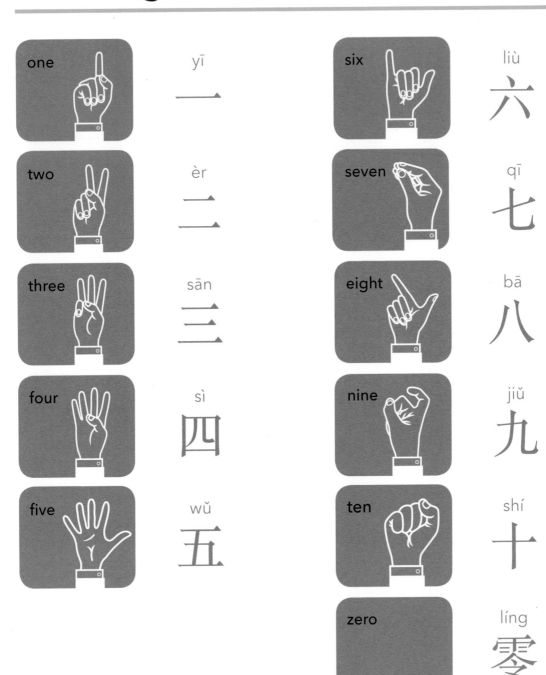

one	yī	一
two	èr	二
three	sān	三
four	sì	四
five	wǔ	五
six	liù	六
seven	qī	七
eight	bā	八
nine	jiǔ	九
ten	shí	十
zero	líng	零

year

The origin of 年 is deeply rooted in agriculture. It was initially a verb, with the rather complex meaning of 'achieving a full and successful harvest'. When talking about a specific year, the Chinese will always say each number individually. For instance, they would say 'the year two zero zero five' rather than 'the year two thousand and five'.

e.g. 二零零八年、一九九七年、三年

month, moon

月 means 'month', but also means 'the moon'. This character is also rooted in agriculture, as Chinese farmers to this day still use the lunar calendar to regulate their crops. Unlike other languages, Chinese doesn't have names for specific months. The Chinese simply add the number of the month in front of 月. Both the lunar and solar calendars are currently used in China.

e.g. 七月、九月、这个月

day, sun

The character 日 evolved from an early drawing of the sun. This depicted a circle with a dot in the middle, symbolizing that the sun emitted light. Over time the circle has become a square, and the dot has changed into a line. When talking about a specific date, the Chinese will simply say a number, followed by 日, so that 三日 would be the third of the month.

e.g. 五日、七日、二十二日

week

星期 means 'week'; it can literally be translated as 'star period'. The Chinese say 星期 followed by a number to designate days of the week, for instance 星期二 is Tuesday. The exception is Sunday, which is 星期日.

e.g. 星期二、一个星期

diǎn

点

o'clock

点 means 'dot', which explains the four dots on the bottom part of the character. It is also used to indicate the hours of the day, because they are marked on clocks by dots. It is preceded by numbers to tell the time, as in 十一点 (11 o'clock). The Chinese use a 12-hour am/pm system, rather than a 24-hour system.

e.g. 五点、七点三十五

jǐ

几

How many?

几 is a question word used to enquire about quantity and numbers. It can best be translated as 'how many?' It is also used to ask the time. 'What time is it?' becomes 现在几点, which is literally translated as 'now, how many hours (have passed)?'

e.g.
几点、几月、几日

fēn

分

minute

The character 分 is made up of 八, which originally meant 'to divide' (and now means 8) and 刀, which means 'knife'. It currently has several meanings, including 'to divide' and 'minute', the idea being that a minute is a small subdivision of an hour. 分 is preceded by a number to indicate the number of minutes past the hour. For instance, 12.30 is expressed as 十二点三十分.

e.g. 一点十二分、三点二十分

When talking about the date, make sure you use 'year + month + date' format.

shí

时

hòu

候

moment

时候 on its own can be translated as 'moment'. It is often used in conjunction with other characters to form new meanings: 什么时候 means 'when?', literally 'what moment?' and ... 的时候 is the indicative when ('When the saints go marching in').

e.g. 的时候、
什么时候

tiān

天

day

The base meaning of 天 is 'sky'. However, the meaning has extended to 'day'. This change comes from the change in the sky from night to day. The character can be combined with either of the modifiers 明(ming), 今 (jin) or 昨 (zuo) to create 昨天 (yesterday)', 今天 (today) or 明天 (tomorrow).

e.g. 昨天、今天、明天

wǔ

午

noon

The character 午 simply designates when the sun is in the middle of the sky (11am–1pm). It has to be combined with either 上 (shang), 中 (zhong) or 下 (xia) to indicate different times of day: 上午 means 'morning', 中午 is 'midday', and 下午 is 'afternoon'.

e.g. 上午、中午、下午

xiàn   zài

现在

now

现在 is made up of 现', which means 'the present' and 在', which can mean 'existing', but is mostly used as 'at' (as in 'at the beach'). Together they mean 'now', as in 'existing in the present'.

e.g. 现在几点、现在是

Exploring the Language

Let's have a look at how to talk about time. First, in a Chinese sentence, the time comes immediately after the subject and always before the action. This is because the Chinese do not use conjugation, relying instead on context. The system for telling the time is quite straightforward and logical. It uses a very simple method of combining numbers with key characters. Instead of saying 'January', 'September' or 'Friday', The Chinese simply say, 'month 1', 'month 9' and 'weekday 5'.

Time phrase to indicate date.

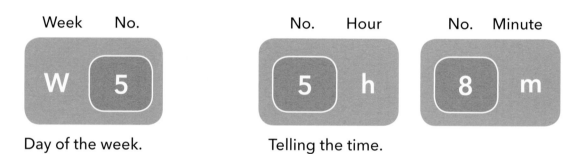

Day of the week.   Telling the time.

For example:

Today is June 3rd.

What is the date today?

jīn tiān jǐ yuè jǐ rì
今天几月几日？

jīn tiān liù yuè sān rì
今天六月三日。

míng tiān xīng qī jǐ
明天星期几？

míng tiān xīng qī wǔ
明天星期五。

Longlong
& Xiongmao
in China

xiàn zài jǐ diǎn
现在几点？

xiàn zài xià wǔ sān diǎn sì shí fēn
现在下午三点四十分。

Practice Time

Using what we have learned in this chapter as a guide, try and find out the hidden words in this word maze. There are 14 in total.

You can go horizontally, vertically or diagonally. Good luck!

yī 一	shí 时	hòu 候	jīn 今	tiān 天
yuè 月	bā 八	jǐ 几	zuó 昨	míng 明
liù 六	diǎn 点	èr 二	shí 十	fēn 分
shàng 上	xīng 星	qī 期	sì 四	jiǔ 九
wǔ 午	xiàn 现	zài 在	diǎn 点	nián 年

1. 8 o'clock
2. Thursday
3. The year 1824
4. Yesterday
5. Today
6. Tomorrow
7. January
8. August
9. 6.20
10. Morning
11. Now
12. What time?
13. Moment
14. 9 years

Basic Characters

 日

day

The earliest version of this character consisted of a circle with a line or dot in the middle. It was meant to represent the sun with the line or dot in the centre symbolizing the emission of light. Over the years it has evolved into a more abstract shape.

Evolution of pictographic characters:

月

moon

In the early days of Chinese writing there were two versions of this character, a circular one and a crescent-shaped one. The crescent shape was quickly adopted to differentiate it from the sun pictogram. It also featured a line in the centre, as ancient Chinese people believed that the moon, like the sun, also emitted light.

Evolution of pictographic characters:

The Dragon Boat Festival

lóng
龙
zhōu
舟
jié
节

Along with Spring Festival and the mid-autumn Lantern Festival, the Dragon Boat Festival (龙舟节) is one of the most important events in the Chinese calendar. It takes place every year on the fifth day of the fifth month in the lunar calendar and celebrates the beginning of the wet season. The Dragon Boat Festival therefore has its roots firmly in agriculture, as the wet season has always been an important time for crops in rural China. Harvests all over the country depend on sufficiently plentiful rainfall during the wet season.

Unlike the Western dragon, which is more traditionally associated with fire, the Chinese dragon is culturally representative of thunder and lightning, clouds and rain. This is why the festival features the famous Dragon Boat race in order to praise and worship these mythical creatures.

As well as being a prayer to the mighty dragons, the Dragon Boat race also commemorates the death of the poet and minister Qu Yuan (屈原) during the Warring States period (475-221 BCE). Qu Yuan came from the state of Chu, and campaigned heavily for reforms that would help bring peace to the country. However, after being slandered and defamed by the state's corrupt financial elite, he was forced into exile. During his time away his mental and physical health began to deteriorate and this worsened when he learned of the capture of the state capital in 278 BCE. When his despair became too much to bear, he threw himself in the Mi Luo River, with a heavy rock tied to his legs. Upon witnessing Qu Yuan's attempt to end his life, the townsfolk immediately took to their boats and hurried to try and rescue him. Sadly they were all too late and therefore, to honour his soul and make sure he didn't go hungry in the afterlife, the townsfolk threw a type of rice delicacy called Zong Zi (粽子) into the river where his body had sunk.

What do we eat during Dragon Boat Festival?

Zong Zi (粽子) is a traditional delicacy consisting of sticky rice stuffed with a variety of fillings and tied in leaves or bamboo reeds. They can be steamed or boiled, and can be shaped like a cone, a tetrahedron or a cylinder. Nowadays the Chinese eat Zong Zi to commemorate the death of Qu Yuan, but the dish was already being eaten long before that. It was initially consumed to honour gods and ancestors. The Chinese prepare and eat Zong Zi during the Dragon Boat Festival, but many also consume it all year round as a healthy and hearty breakfast or as a snack.

Zong Zi is regarded as a culinary favourite of the entire nation, yet the shape, filling and cooking method can vary greatly from province to province. In general, northerners favour sweeter Zong Zi, filled with beans, nuts or dried fruit, whereas southerners prefer a savoury version, often using various meats and vegetables for the filling. Although quite different, both these approaches make for very tasty Zong Zi!

You will need:

Glutinous rice
Bamboo leaves
Strings/boiled straws
Desired fillings (dates, red bean paste, pork pieces, etc.)
Desired dips (sugar, syrup, etc.)

Stockpot
Scissors

How to make Zong Zi (粽子)

Step 1
Wash the rice, and then boil it for 15-20 mins; alternatively, soak the rice in water for two hours.

Step 2
Carefully, using a pair of scissors, cut the stem of the leaf to make it easier to fold.

Step 3
Fold two leaves into cone shapes, and fill with rice and other ingredients using a spoon.

Step 4
Don't use too much filling, leave a little space at the top to make folding later easier.

Step 5
While maintaining a pyramid shape at the bottom, fold in the top and make sure it is tight.

Step 6
Wrap up the Zong Zi completely and then tie it either using string or boiled straw.

Step 7
Put the Zong Zi in a pot of boiling water, making sure they are fully submerged. Boil for 2-3 hours.

Step 8
When they have finished boiling, place in cold water to cool. To serve, unwrap the Zong Zi and dip in sugar or other sauces.

jiàn

见

miàn

面

Encounters

This chapter focuses on interacting with others and introducing oneself. We will start by learning several useful daily phrases such as 'Hello', 'Thank you' or 'Don't mention it'. We'll also learn how adding one simple character can easily turn any sentence into a 'yes' or 'no' question. Next we will move on to introduce Chinese modifiers and learn a couple of easy and useful ones. Then we'll introduce sentences to help you ask people about themselves, such as 'How old are you?' or 'What's your name?' This chapter should equip you with the tools needed for polite day-to-day conversation.

Building Blocks

These short phrases are essential for daily communication in Chinese.
They will help you deal with all kinds of situations in a polite and courteous way.

hello!

nǐ hǎo
你好

good-bye!

zài jiàn
再见

thanks!

xiè xie
谢谢

don't mention it.

bú kè qì
不客气

sorry!

duì bù qǐ
对不起

it's alright!

méi guān xì
没关系

ma

吗

yes/no?

吗 is a word added at the end of a sentence to turn it into a yes or no question. 你喜欢咖啡 is 'You like coffee'. But 你喜欢咖啡吗? is 'Do you like coffee?'

e.g. 好吗、是吗

ne

呢

what about?

呢 is a question word put at the end of a sentence to turn it into a reciprocal question. For instance: 'Today's not good. What about tomorrow?' in Chinese would be 今天不好，明天呢?

e.g. 你呢、明天呢

hǎo

好

good, well

好 is a very useful character that means 'good' or 'well'. It is combined with 你 to give 你好, which means 'hello' (you good). It comprises two radicals: the first is 女, which means 'female', the second is 子, which means 'male'. This dates back to ancient China, when a marriage was always considered a joyful and fruitful occasion.

e.g. 好吗、很好、太好、不好

hěn

很

very

很 can be translated as the English word 'very'. Just like in English, it can be used with adjectives and adverbs, such as 好 or 大 to amplify them. However it can also be used in conjunction with actions, where the meaning becomes 'really'. For instance, 我很喜欢 ('I really like …')

e.g. 很好、很不好、不很好

tài

太

too

太 is similar to 很, although much stronger. It can most closely be likened to the English word 'too' (as in too much). However it doesn't have any negative connotations when used with positive words. 很好 is 'very good', 太好 is 'brilliant'! Similarly, 很不好 is 'very bad', but 太不好 means 'awful'.

e.g. 太好、太不好 、不太好

gāo xìng

高兴

happy

rèn shì

认识

to know

qǐng

请

please

wèi

喂

hello!
(on the phone)

míng zì

名字

name

This vocabulary is especially useful for when meeting people for the first time and you find yourself having to introduce yourself and ask about others.

to call

叫 literally means 'to call'. It is used when asking or indicating what something is called, or what someone's name is. For example, 她叫 Jane ('Her name is Jane'). It can be used to give either a full name or just a surname.

e.g. 我叫、我爸爸叫、先生叫

years old

岁 is a character to help give a person's age, similar to the English 'years old'. It is made up of 山, which means 'mountain' and 夕, which means 'sunset'. You might imagine a beautiful sunset over the mountain, marking the passing of the years. For example, 'I'm 21 years old' in Chinese becomes 我二十一岁.

e.g. 几岁、八岁、三十二岁

what?

什么 is a question word, equivalent to 'what' in English. For example, 'What's your name?' in Chinese is 你叫什么 (you're called what?). In a question, the place for 什么 depends on what you are asking about.

e.g. 是什么、叫什么

Exploring the Language

Let's have a look at how we talk about names and age in Chinese. In Chinese, instead of saying 'my name is ...', it is more idiomatic to say, 'I'm called ...' 我叫... If you would like to ask someone's name, use the same sentence structure and simply replace the right part of the sentence with the appropriate question word 什么 (what) as seen in the example below. When talking about age, note that as age is considered descriptive, avoid using 是. For example, in English we say 'He is 16 years old' but in Chinese we say 他十六岁 (He 16 years old).

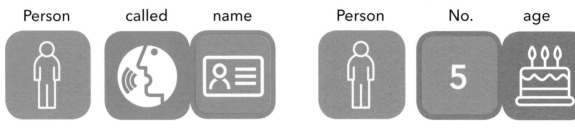

| Person | called | name | | Person | No. | age |

Introducing the name of a person.   Stating the age of a person.

For example:

I'm 24 years old.

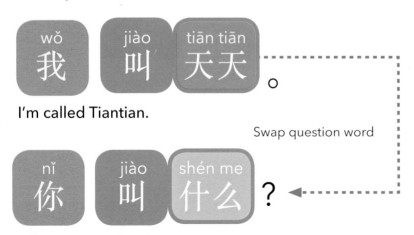

I'm called Tiantian.

Swap question word

What's your name?

你好！你叫什么？
nǐ hǎo nǐ jiào shén me

你好，我叫龙龙。你呢？
nǐ hǎo wǒ jiào lóng long nǐ ne

我叫熊猫。
wǒ jiào xióng māo

你几岁？
nǐ jǐ suì

Longlong
& Xiongmao
in China

我九岁，你几岁？
wǒ jiǔ suì nǐ jǐ suì

我十岁。
wǒ shí suì

我很高兴认识你！
wǒ hěn gāo xìng rèn shi nǐ

我也很高兴认识你！
wǒ yě hěn gāo xìng rèn shi nǐ

Practice Time

Using what we have learned in this chapter as a guide,
try and match the question with the appropriate answer.

When you're in China, you'll hear these
basic phrases everywhere. Can you figure
out what they're saying?

nǐ 你	jiào 叫	shén me 什么

zài jiàn 再见

zài jiàn 再见

wǒ 我 | bā 八 | suì 岁

nǐ hǎo 你好 | ma 吗

bú kè qì 不客气

duì bù qǐ 对不起

wǒ 我 | jiào 叫 | tiān tiān 天天

nǐ 你 | jǐ 几 | suì 岁

wǒ 我 | hěn 很 | hǎo 好

xiè xie 谢谢

méi guān xì 没关系

Basic Characters

good,
well

好 is made up of 女 and 子, the radicals for 'female' and 'male' brought together. In its earliest form, this character depicted a woman kneeling down, and a man or infant on the right. It symbolized a man and a woman brought together in marriage, or the birth of a child.

Evolution of pictographic characters:

too

The character 太 is based on 大, which means 'big'. By adding an extra stroke on the bottom part, the character symbolizes that it is bigger than big, hence the meaning of 'too (much)'. This was already the case in the earlier versions of this character.

Evolution of pictographic characters:

Chinese Philosophies and Thinkers

zhōng
中

guó
国

guó
国

xué
学

China has a rich history of great thinkers and philosophers that dates back thousands of years. Many historians consider Chinese philosophy to have been born in the Spring and Autumn periods and the Warring States period (although certain elements of Chinese philosophy predate these periods). These periods correspond to the 7th–3rd centuries BCE, which, interestingly, is around the same time that Greek philosophy was beginning to flourish.

The Warring States period was a time of great chaos and turmoil during which many local lords fought against one another to gain control of an entire region. To gain strength and power, they broke with the aristocratic system that had previously been in place and began to recruit commoners. It was the first time in history that common people had access to education and were given political influence, which led to the rise of many intellectuals. Many challenges arose as a result of constant societal upheavals and a rapidly rising population. Consequently, thinkers constructed many ideologies and political systems to deal with these issues.

These philosophies were known as 诸子百家 (the Hundred Schools of Thought). Despite the name, there were in fact over 1,000 ideologies and theories being discussed during this period. Many of these have, up to the present day, had a considerable influence on Chinese culture, as well as on East Asian culture as a whole. This period culminated in the unification of the country, and the establishment of the Qin dynasty.

Among the thousands of thinkers that were active during the Spring and Autumn and Warring States periods, three have been particularly influential, and continue to be studied and followed to this day, both in China and in the rest of the world.

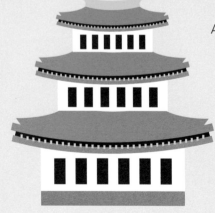

孔子
Confucius

Confucianism is the name given to the theories and teachings of the Chinese philosopher Confucius. The name Confucius is actually an Anglicization of the Chinese 孔丘 (Kong Qiu). Born in 551 BCE during the Warring States period, he was educated in a school for commoners. However, he took advantage of the fluctuating geopolitical situation of the time to gain influence over the local aristocracy. His teachings are now widely read and followed both inside and outside China. Confucian philosophy notably champions personal and governmental morality, family loyalty and ancestor veneration, and emphasizes the importance of rigid rituals and social order. On top of discussing ethics and morals, Confucius also wrote on religious beliefs and principles, and is considered a deity in Taoism.

老子
Lao Zi

In Chinese, the words 老子 (Lao Zi) can be translated as 'old master', and is in itself an honoured title. It is believed that Lao Zi's original name would have been either Li Er or Li Dan. Lao Zi is an important and prominent figure in Chinese philosophy and religion. He is considered to be the founder of philosophical Taoism and is a traditional deity of religious Taoism and of other Chinese religions. Lao Zi is regarded as the author of the *Daodejing*, which is one of the most translated books in the world, second only to the Bible. It is considered an important work in traditional Chinese cosmogony and philosophy. The *Daodejing* introduces the Dao or Tao as the source and ideal state of all things in existence. A central concept of the *Daodejing* is also 无为 (wu wei), or 'non-action', which involves respecting the natural flow and balance of the universe.

孟子
Mencius

Mencius was a very influential and prominent philosopher of the Warring States period and is considered the most important Confucian thinker after Confucius himself. Like Confucius, Mencius' name is an Anglicization of the Chinese name 孟子 (Meng Zi). It is believed that he was a pupil of Zisi, Confucius' grandson, which prompted him to develop and interpret Confucian ideas. Mencius explored the subject of human nature, and asserted the innate goodness of the individual. He believed that evil and bad moral character was the result of societal influence and its lack of a positive cultivating influence. During the course of his life, Mencius travelled widely and conversed with many kings of the time. His dialogues with rulers were recorded and compiled in a book called *Mencius,* which had considerable influence on the Neo-Confucians of the Song dynasty (960–1279 CE).

chū

出

xíng

行

Going Places

In this chapter, we will learn how to talk about going to different places. We'll start with several common means of transport and two key words that can be used with them, which covers how we interact with these means of transport. We'll then move on to introducing several useful locations, along with three more key verbs that can be used in combination with these places. By the end of this chapter, we will be able to construct useful and complex sentences involving transport and travel. When you are travelling in China, being able to use these basic sentences will definitely come in handy.

Building Blocks

taxi

The word for 'taxi' in Chinese is a recently invented word. The word 出租 means 'rental' and the word 车 means 'car'.
e.g. 坐出租车、出租车来了

bus

The word literally means 'public car'. 公交 has the meaning of 'public service'. Therefore 公交车 is a car to be shared by the public.
e.g. 开公交车、坐公交车

train

火 is the character for 'fire'. So the word 火车 literally means 'fire vehicle'. The word comes from old steam engine trains.
e.g. 坐火车、上火车

boat

The word now means either a boat, a ship, or a ferry. The character combines 舟, which means boat and 公, which means 'public'.
e.g. 开船、大船

plane

A plane is essentially a flying machine, and that's exactly what we call it in Chinese!
飞 means 'to fly' and 机 is a machine.
e.g. 坐飞机、开飞机

Travelling in China? Afraid of getting lost? Let's start with learning some common means of transportation.

kāi
开

to drive

The 开 has several meanings. The character originally meant to open something, however it has adapted to the modern world and now it also means to turn on electrical equipment. In this chapter, we see it extends its meaning to 'drive' a car, a boat or a plane.

e.g. 开车、开出租车、开飞机

zuò
坐

to take

The 坐 word looks like two people sitting on two back-to-back seats. From this we can deduce that originally it meant 'to sit'. Like the previous character, it has adapted. Nowadays it also means to be a passenger on a transportation system, very similar to the verb 'to take' (the bus) in English.

e.g. 坐出租车、坐公交车

zěn me

怎么

how?

This word is very similar to the word 'how' in English. It also means 'how is' and 'how about'. Unlike English, in Chinese it doesn't have to appear at the beginning of a sentence, it appears where the answer part of the sentence should be.

e.g. 怎么去、怎么来

home

The character 家 means both 'home' and 'family'. This character's top part looks like a roof, which signifies that everyone in a family shares a roof.

e.g. 回家、去你家

school

The word 学校 means 'school'. 学 on its own means to 'study'. In combination with the character 校 it means 'a place to study'.

e.g. 去学校、来学校

restaurant

The word 饭馆 means 'restaurant'. The character 饭 means 'food' or 'rice', and the character 馆 has the meaning of a public place.

e.g. 在饭馆、和你们去饭馆

shop

The word 商店 means 'shop'. 商 has the connotation of 'commerce' and 店 denotes a place where trade activities may take place.

e.g. 去商店、在商店买东西

train station

The word 火车 站 combines 火车, which means 'train' and 站, which means 'station'. 站 could be used with other words such as 公交站.

e.g. 在火车站坐火车

hospital

The word 医院 means 'hospital'. The character 医 has a lot to do with medicine and doctors, while 院 means 'courtyard' or 'institution'.

e.g. 来医院、开车去医院

Can you learn these words for places in Chinese? They can be used with the verbs on the right side. Good luck!

qù

去

to go

The character 去 means to go. It originally looked like a person walking. It has changed over time, but we can still see a little bit of legs and arms moving. It is a very important word to learn as it can be used with most place words.
e.g. 去商店、去我家、去火车站

nǎ   er

哪儿

Where?

The word 哪儿 means 'where'. When constructing a question, it could be used in the answer part of a sentence. In the north of China, people usually use 哪儿 whereas in the south, people prefer to use the expression 哪里 instead.

ie. 去哪儿、来哪儿

lái

来

to come

The character is a combination of a 'tree' and two 'person' building blocks. In ancient China, 'to come' was represented by the old character for wheat, which had been brought from Europe. The traditional form is 來.
e.g. 来饭店、坐出租车来

huí

回

to return

The character 回 means 'to return'. It is a combination of a small 口, which means 'mouth' and a big 口, which means 'to surround'. You might imagine that it depicts a swirling whirlpool, continuously turning back on itself.
e.g. 回家、回学校、开车回

Exploring the Language

Let's have a look at how to construct sentences in Chinese. Unlike many letter-based languages, we don't need tenses or conjugation to express time. We just specify the time and put it immediately after the subject. As well as not having to conjugate verbs, we do not change sentence structures when constructing questions. All we have to do is replace what we want to ask with the appropriate question word as shown in the example below. These two rules make Chinese grammar very easy to grasp.

Subject	Time	Action one		Action two	
person	time	take	transport	go	place

For example:

wǒ 我　zuò 坐　huǒ chē 火车　qù 去　běi jīng 北京 。

I am taking the train to Beijing.

wǒ 我　míng tiān zǎo shang 明天早上　zuò 坐　huǒ chē 火车　qù 去　běi jīng 北京

I'm going to take the train to Beijing tomorrow morning.

Swap question word

nǐ 你　míng tiān zǎo shang 明天早上　zěn me 怎么　qù 去　běi jīng 北京 ？

How are you going to Beijing tomorrow morning?

龙龙你好,你今天去哪儿?
lóng long nǐ hǎo nǐ jīn tiān qù nǎ er

熊猫你好,我今天去商店。
xióng māo nǐ hǎo wǒ jīn tiān qù shāng diàn

你今天什么时候去商店?
nǐ jīn tiān shén me shí hòu qù shāng diàn

我今天下午去商店。
wǒ jīn tiān xià wǔ qù shāng diàn

Longlong & Xiongmao in China

你今天下午怎么去商店?
nǐ jīn tiān xià wǔ zěn me qù shāng diàn

我坐公交车去商店。
wǒ zuò gōng jiāo chē qù shāng diàn

我和你去,好吗?
wǒ hé nǐ qù hǎo ma

太好了,再见!
tài hǎo le zài jiàn

Practice Time

Using what we have learned in this chapter as a guide, try and reorganize these vocabulary cards into the correct order to form a sentence. The colours will help you determine what the function of the word is.

It's time to travel! Let's learn how to describe going from place to place.

Yesterday he went to China by plane.

zuó tiān xià wǔ	qù	zhōng guó	tā	zuò	fēi jī
昨天下午	去	中国	他	坐	飞机

① ② ③ ④

How will you come to Beijing in the morning at 8am?

zěn me	zǎo shang bā diǎn	nǐ	lái	běi jīng
怎么	早上八点	你	来	北京

① ② ③ ④

Basic Characters

去
to go

The character is a combination of 'private' and 'soil'. It alludes to a person leaving a place to go somewhere. Originally found on oracle bones as shown underneath, the character resembled a person walking away, and meant leaving where one lives and going somewhere else.

Evolution of pictographic characters:

来
to come

This character is a combination of 'tree' and two people. In ancient China, 'to come' was represented by a character meaning 'wheat', which had been brought to China from Europe. They named this vital crop 'food coming from outside'. The meaning has changed a lot since then.

Evolution of pictographic characters:

Chinese Scenery

zhōng
中

guó
国

měi
美

jǐng
景

西湖
West Lake

China has 21 national parks that contain lakes. Among these 西湖 (Xi Hu), also known as 'West Lake', is the most famous. West Lake is a freshwater lake situated in the middle of Hangzhou, the capital of the Zhejiang province. Its beauty and serene grace have been a source of inspiration for many Chinese poets and painters throughout the centuries. It has also greatly influenced traditional Chinese garden design. West Lake features many historic temples, gardens, pagodas and even artificial islands. Springtime brings green leaves and beautiful blossom, while in the summer the lake is filled with lotus flowers. The calm skies of autumn make it the perfect place to enjoy the sight of the moon during the mid-autumn festival, and in winter pristine layers of the whitest snow cover the trees and the bridges. West Lake is a place that combines classical Chinese architecture with the country's astounding natural landscapes. Above all, it has been a cradle of Chinese culture, poetry and philosophy for many years.

少林寺
Shaolin Monastery

The Shaolin Monastery, or Shaolin Si (少林寺), is arguably the most famous temple in China. It is located near the base of Mount Song near the city of Deng Feng in Henan province, and is classified as a World Heritage Site by UNESCO. It is known today as a place where visitors can go to witness amazing martial arts demonstrations and learn about Chinese Chan Buddhism. The style of martial arts and of meditation practised at the Shaolin Si has been exported throughout Asia and has heavily influenced the fighting styles and religions of Korea and Japan. It was first built in the 5th century CE as a place of peace and prayer by an Indian monk named Batuo, whose teachings were favoured by Emperor Xiao Wen. Shaolin monks started practising martial arts towards the end of the Sui dynasty, which was a time of turmoil for the whole country. The monks learned how to fight as a means of defending themselves against frequent bandit raids.

Travelling to China? These amazing sites that combine nature with Chinese culture should not be missed!

泰山
Mount Tai

There are five sacred mountains (五岳) in China that have very significant historical value. Tai shan or Mount Tai (泰山) is often considered the most important. 泰 in Chinese carries the meaning of stability and peace. Throughout history, Mount Tai was frequently chosen by emperors as a place to hold lavish ceremonies, where the court would pray to the heavens and thank them for peace and prosperity. Featuring grandeur, grace, risk, mystery and wonder, the majesty of Mount Tai has moved and inspired many visitors over the years. The mountain is now filled with relics from different periods, from Taoist temples to Ming-style building complexes. Mount Tai is also well known for the breathtaking sunrise that can be seen from its peak. Many travellers climb up the mountain steps carved into the rock overnight to marvel at the sight of the sea of clouds illuminated by the rising sun.

gòu

购

wù

物

Shopping

This chapter is all about food and drink; the vocabulary we will learn is based on everyday dishes, ingredients and drinks common to Western and Asian cuisines. We'll also learn various verbs that can be used to convey liking or wanting something. Later we will approach the subject of ordering or shopping for food. We'll learn about the Chinese currency and how to enquire about the price of a product. Vocabulary will cover useful words such as 'expensive' and 'cheap', or 'buy' and 'sell'. By the end of the chapter we'll be able to order Chinese food, express how delicious (or not) we found it and, most importantly, haggle with the waiter!

Building Blocks

mǐ fàn
米饭

rice

米饭 means 'cooked rice'. 米 is the uncooked rice plant and 饭 means 'meal'.
e.g. 吃米饭

cài
菜

vegetables

菜 is both vegetables and 'cooked dishes' (not necessarily vegetarian).
e.g. 吃菜

píng guǒ
苹果

apple

苹果 is an apple. The character 果 means 'fruit'.
e.g. 吃苹果

jī dàn
鸡蛋

egg

鸡 means 'chicken' and 蛋 means 'egg'. The Chinese always specify what type of egg they mean and do the same for milk.
e.g. 吃鸡蛋

shuǐ
水

water

水 means 'water'. The character is meant to look like three streams, and was initially meant to look like a waterfall.
e.g. 喝水

chá
茶

tea

茶 is tea, which China is very famous for! The top radical is 艹 meaning 'plant', the middle is 人 (people) and the bottom one is 水 (water).
e.g. 喝茶

kā fēi
咖啡

coffee

咖啡 is a recent word, as coffee was not introduced to China until the late 19th century. The word is a sound translation of the English word 'coffee'.
e.g. 喝咖啡

niú nǎi
牛奶

milk

牛 is cow, and 奶 is milk. Just as with eggs, the Chinese always specify what type of milk they mean.
e.g. 喝牛奶

The building blocks opposite can be combined with the ones below to create phrases related to food.

chī

吃

to eat
The character 吃 means 'to eat'. The radical on the left means 'mouth', and the one on the right means 'air'. 吃 originally meant 'to stutter', or 'to have trouble breathing', and later evolved into 'to eat'. 吃 is applicable to all edible solids, including medicine.
e.g. 吃苹果、吃鸡蛋、不吃

hē

喝

to drink
喝 means 'to drink'. Just as for 吃 (above) there is the radical for 'mouth' on the left-hand side, whereas on the right, we can see the radical for 'shout', which indicates the pronunciation. 喝 is applicable to any kind of ingestible liquid, and is also used for soup or yoghurt.
e.g. 喝水、喝咖啡、不喝

xiē

些

some
些, or 一些 can both be translated as 'some', as in 一些苹果, which means 'some apples'. 些 is considered a measure word in Chinese.

buy

The character 买 means 'to buy'. 头 here means 'head', as in ancient China, animal trading was one of the most important trades.
e.g. 买吃的、买东西

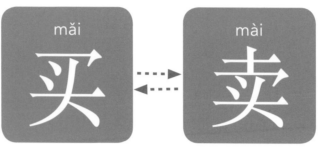

sell

卖 is very similar to the character that has the opposite meaning – 买. It has an extra 十 on top of it. However it doesn't share the same tone as 买.
e.g. 卖东西、卖苹果

money

钱 is the character for money. The left radical 钅 means 'gold', and the right part 戋 means 'to kill', or 'to fight for something'. Therefore this character actually means 'to kill for wealth'.
e.g. 多少钱、有钱

things

In this word, 东 means 'east', 洗 means 'west', so 东西 literally means 'east-west'. Now it has evolved into meaning 'things or objects'.
e.g. 买东西、什么东西

块 means 'a piece (of something)' as in 一块苹果 (a piece of apple). It is also a very common colloquial word for a unit of Chinese currency (yuan).

e.g. 一块四、八块钱

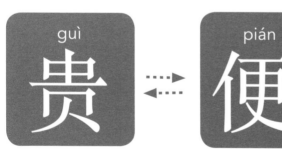

expensive   cheap

duō shǎo

多少

how many?

多少 means 'how many?', it is an alternative to 几 (see page 32) and is often used when enquiring about quantity or price. 多 means 'many', and 少 means 'few'. 你吃多少个苹果 (how many apples did you eat?)

e.g. 有多少、买多少、多少钱

think, want to do

The basic meaning of 想 is 'to think'. However, when followed by an action, the meaning extends to 'to want to do something'. For instance 我想鸡蛋 is 'I think about eggs' whereas 我想吃鸡蛋 is 'I want to eat eggs'.

e.g. 想吃、想喝、想买

to love

The character 爱 means 'to love'. 爱 is much stronger than 喜欢 and would almost never be used for people. It is to be used with care, as it has very strong connotations. Originally the character included the radical 心, which means 'heart', signifying strong feelings. However, this radical has disappeared from the simplified version of the character.

e.g. 爱吃菜、爱买、不爱

to like

Both 喜 and 欢 were originally used to describe feelings of joy and happiness. Nowadays the two have been put together to mean 'to like'. For instance 我很喜欢苹果 is 'I really like apples'.

e.g. 喜欢米饭、喜欢牛奶

Exploring the Language

Let's have a look at how to talk about what we want and need in Chinese. As we have seen before in previous chapters, a simple sentence is subject + action. In this case we could add a modal action (such as like, want etc.) before the main action to complement it. For example, 'I like eating apples' is 我喜欢吃苹果. We could also add a time word to specify when the action is taking place. However, make sure the time word comes after the subject and before the action.

person	modal	verb	object		person	time	verb	object

Someone's feeling about doing something.

Someone does something at a certain time.

For example:

   。

I like eating apples.

   。

I'm going to buy apples tomorrow.

  ?

How much are the apples?

nǐ hǎo nǐ jīn tiān xiǎng mǎi shén me
你好，你今天想买什么？

wǒ xiǎng mǎi píng guǒ nǐ ne
我想买苹果，你呢？

wǒ xiǎng mǎi cài hé jī dàn nǐ xǐ huān píng guǒ ma
我想买菜和鸡蛋，你喜欢苹果吗？

wǒ hěn xǐ huān píng guǒ nǐ ne
我很喜欢苹果，你呢？

Longlong & Xiongmao in China

wǒ yě hěn xǐ huān píng guǒ
我也很喜欢苹果！

píng guǒ duō shǎo qián
苹果多少钱？

píng guǒ yī kuài qián hěn pián yì
苹果一块钱，很便宜！

tài hǎo le wǒ mǎi wǔ ge píng guǒ
太好了！我买五个苹果。

Practice Time

Using what we have learned in this chapter as a guide, try and help these people find their favourite food.

These people all have their own preferred food. Can you help them to find the correct ones for them?

wǒ 我	xǐ huan 喜欢
chī 吃	jī dàn 鸡蛋

。

wǒ 我	xǐ huan 喜欢
hē 喝	niú nǎi 牛奶

。

wǒ 我	xǐ huan 喜欢
chī 吃	píng guǒ 苹果

。

wǒ 我	xǐ huan 喜欢
hē 喝	kā fēi 咖啡

。

Basic Characters

吃

to eat

吃 is made up of two radicals, 口, which means 'mouth' and 气, which means 'air'. The early drawing of a mouth is easily recognizable on the first version of this character. The top part, even in the early days, was more abstract and was meant to look like the wind blowing.

Evolution of pictographic characters:

米

rice

The pictogram for rice was originally intended to look like a rice plant, the middle line representing the stem and the perpendicular lines sprouting florets. It evolved in this way because of an early copying mistake. The central vertical line was supposed to be separated by the horizontal line.

Evolution of pictographic characters:

Eight Chinese Culinary Traditions

bā
八

dà
大

cài
菜

xì
系

China is a civilization with over 5,000 years of history. Chinese food and cooking techniques are one of the most important parts of its culture. Modern Chinese food has benefitted from centuries of development. The country has a varied landscape with several different climate zones, which have long provided talented chefs with a wide variety of ingredients. Using techniques that have been perfected over millennia, the Chinese have invented over 10,000 different regional culinary traditions. Chinese cuisine has not only affected and influenced the cooking styles of other Asian countries, it has also been exported to the West, to become one of the most consumed and celebrated cuisines in the world. Among the myriad of different local cuisines, eight stand out as particularly unique and influential. Visitors from the four corners of the world travel to these eight provinces to experience their dishes.

Sichuan Cuisine
Sichuan chefs have a saying: 'one dish has one flavour; one hundred dishes have one hundred flavours'. Sichuan dishes are famous for their tangy spiciness, full-bodied flavours and their deep, rustic culinary background.

Guangdong (or Cantonese) Cuisine
Unlike Sichuan dishes that rely heavily on spices and oils, Guangdong dishes are better known for bringing out the natural flavours of their meat and vegetables. It is the style of Chinese food most commonly found outside of China.

Zhejiang Cuisine
The capital of the Zhejiang region, the city of Hangzhou, is nicknamed 'The Venice of the Orient'. Its cuisine comprises a variety of esoteric seafood, such as sea cucumbers and various marine plants, all served with fresh seasonal vegetables.

The cuisines of China are famous around the world. Do you know that there are eight main culinary traditions?

Jiangsu Cuisine

Presentation is of paramount importance in Jiangsu cuisine, as it was originally developed for imperial banquets. Jiangsu is a coastal province, and its cuisine features many fragrant seafood dishes and a variety of fish soups.

Fujian Cuisine

The cuisine of the Fujian region is famous for its sweet-and-sour flavours and its use of fresh ingredients from mountains and rivers. The province is best known for its 'drunken' dishes, which have mouth-watering red colours and strong, fragrant smells.

Hunan Cuisine

Just like Sichuan, the Hunan province is famous for its spicy dishes and careful combination of ingredients. However it is not as mouth-numbing. The cuisine from this region features a variety of sautéed vegetables, rich and spicy stir-fries and smoked meats.

Anhui Cuisine

The Anhui region is surrounded by mountains and forests. The local cuisine uses many wild plants and animals specific to its surroundings. It's known for its hearty peasant food with dark, bold flavours and rustic cooking methods, such as wood fire stoves.

Shandong Cuisine

Shandong was one of the earliest inhabited regions of China, and its cooking style has influenced many of the surrounding provinces. It's the oldest cuisine in the country and has the most varied range of ingredients, featuring many different meats, fishes and local vegetables.

zài

jiā

At Home

This chapter covers different areas of the home and how to describe locations around it. The vocabulary includes a variety of objects one might find around the house as well as family pets. We will also learn positioning words, such as 'on top of' or 'on the left'. A key part of this lesson will be tackling the sentence structures necessary to combine the vocabulary with these positioning words. This will be very useful if you want to state clearly where one object is in relation to another. Furthermore, the grammar learned in this chapter will help prepare you for later lessons in this book.

Building Blocks

cat

猫 means 'cat'. The radical 犭 on the left means 'animal' and is found in most animal characters.
e.g. 喜欢猫、猫在哪儿

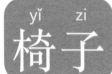

dog

狗 means 'dog'. Just as for 猫 you can find the 犭 radical on the left.
e.g. 他的狗、爱狗

table

桌子 is table. The bottom part of 桌 contains the radical 木, which means 'wood'.
e.g. 买桌子、桌子在

chair

椅 also contains the radical 木. This dates back to ancient times when all furniture was made of wood.
e.g. 有椅子、椅子是"

TV

电视 means 'TV'. The character 电 means 'electricity' and 视 means 'vision'.
e.g. 电视在、三个电视

computer

The character 脑 stands for 'brain', therefore 电脑 literally means 'electric brain'.
e.g. 电脑、有电脑

clothes

衣服 means 'clothes'. 衣 was originally a drawing of a jacket. It has evolved over the years.
e.g. 衣服在哪儿、我的衣服

cup

杯子 is equivalent to either 'mug', 'cup' or 'glass'. It refers to all drinking utensils.
e.g. 一个杯子、这个杯子

to be at/in

在 can be translated as either ' to be at' or 'to be in'. Its original meaning was 'to exist' or 'to be alive'. Now it is commonly used to specify locations. For instance, 我在家 would be translated as 'I'm at home'. 在 is considered a verb in the sentence, there is no need to use 是 (see page 18).

e.g. 在哪儿、在商店、不在

to live, to stay

住 means 'to live (somewhere)' or 'to stay (somewhere)' It is made of the radicals 亻, which comes directly from the character 人, and 主, which means 'host' or 'master (of a home)'. For instance 我住在北京 is translated as 'I live in Beijing'.

e.g. 住在他们家、不住在

where?

The word 哪儿 means 'where'. When constructing a question, it could be used in the answer part of a sentence. In the north of China, people usually use 哪儿, whereas in the south, people prefer to use the expression 哪里 instead.

e.g. 在哪儿、住哪儿

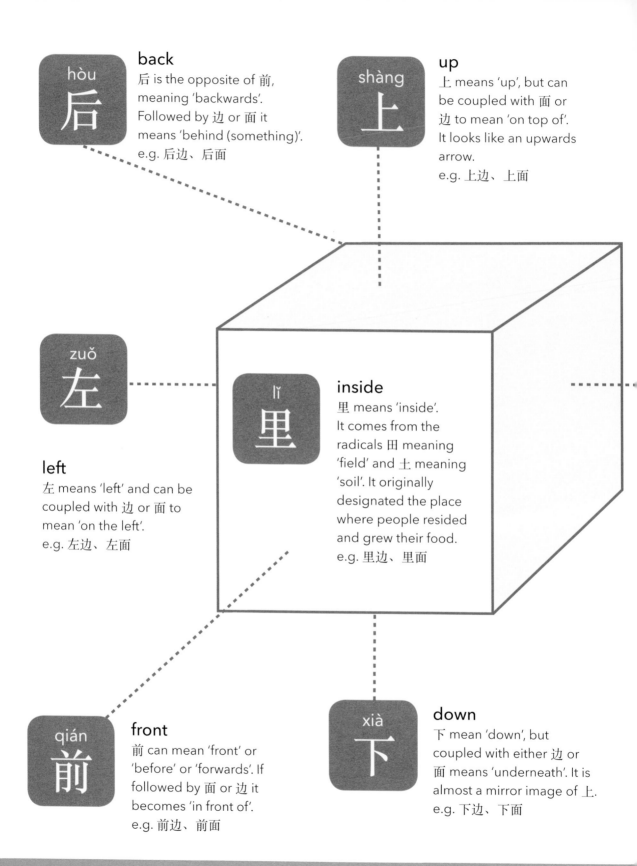

back
hòu
后

后 is the opposite of 前, meaning 'backwards'. Followed by 边 or 面 it means 'behind (something)'.
e.g. 后边、后面

up
shàng
上

上 means 'up', but can be coupled with 面 or 边 to mean 'on top of'. It looks like an upwards arrow.
e.g. 上边、上面

left
zuǒ
左

左 means 'left' and can be coupled with 边 or 面 to mean 'on the left'.
e.g. 左边、左面

inside
lǐ
里

里 means 'inside'. It comes from the radicals 田 meaning 'field' and 土 meaning 'soil'. It originally designated the place where people resided and grew their food.
e.g. 里边、里面

front
qián
前

前 can mean 'front' or 'before' or 'forwards'. If followed by 面 or 边 it becomes 'in front of'.
e.g. 前边、前面

down
xià
下

下 mean 'down', but coupled with either 边 or 面 means 'underneath'. It is almost a mirror image of 上.
e.g. 下边、下面

biān
边

side

The character 边 originally meant 'the edge of a mountain'. The meaning has evolved over the years to simply mean 'side'. It can be coupled with any of the characters from the page on the left to describe positions, for example, 左边 means 'left side' or 在电视左边 means 'on the left side of the TV'.

e.g. 上边、左边、外边、那边

yòu
右

right

右 means 'right' and can be coupled with 边 or 面 to mean 'on the right'.

e.g. 右边、右面

miàn
面

side

The character 面 originally meant 'face' (as in someone's face). It has also recently acquired the meaning 'side' and, in most cases, is interchangeable with 边. For instance, 右面 means 'right side' or 在我右边 is 'on my right side'.

e.g. 里面、下面、右面、后面

wài
外

outside

外 means 'outside' or 'out'. The left side of the character symbolizes the moon and the right side means 'divination'. The character therefore refers to celestial bodies, which are far away from us.

e.g. 外边、外面

Exploring the Language

Let's have a look at how to indicate locations in Chinese. If you want to indicate where something is, you often use a phrase beginning with 在. The simplest form would be 在 followed by the place. For example, 'at home' would be 在家. However, if you want to specify the exact location, simply add a 'direction' word after the object. For example, 'on the table' would be 在桌子上. Also note that in a complex sentence with various elements, the location phrase comes after the time word, but before the action.

Describing the location of an object in relation to another.

For example:

The TV is at home.

Where is the TV?

The TV is on the table.

The TV isn't on the table.

lóng long　nǐ　yǒu　māo　ma
龙龙？你有猫吗

wǒ　yǒu　wǒ　yǒu　xiǎo　māo　hé　xiǎo　gǒu
我有，我有小猫和小狗。

xiǎo　gǒu　zài　nǎ　er
小狗在哪儿？

xiǎo　gǒu　zài　diàn　shì　hòu　mian
小狗在电视后面。

Longlong & Xiongmao in China

xiǎo　māo　zài　nǎ　er
小猫在哪儿？

xiǎo　māo　zài　yǐ　zi　xià　mian
小猫在椅子下面。

xiǎo　māo　xǐ　huan　xiǎo　gǒu　ma
小猫喜欢小狗吗？

hěn　xǐ　huan　tā　men　zhù　zài　zhuō　zi　xià　mian
很喜欢，他们住在桌子下面。

Practice Time

These sentences are all trying to describe what is shown in this picture. Using what we have learned in this chapter as a guide, try to decide if they are true or false.

Be careful, 在 phrases describe the location of the first object in relation to the second one.

1.
diàn nǎo	zài	zhuō zi	shàng bian
电脑	在	桌子	上 边

✔ ✘

2.
gǒu	zài	shuǐ	yòu bian
狗	在	水	右边

✔ ✘

3.
bēi zi	zài	shuǐ	xià bian
杯子	在	水	下边

✔ ✘

4.
gǒu	zài	zhuō zi	shàng bian
狗	在	桌子	上 边

✔ ✘

Basic Characters

在

to be in,
to be at

The left part of the original pictographic version of 在 is meant to represent the beams and supporting columns of early Chinese houses. The right part is an early character for 'soil'. It was evocative of the stability brought by shelter and early agriculture.

Evolution of pictographic characters:

里

in, inside

Just as for 在 we can find the character for 'soil' at the bottom. The top part is 田, which was meant to look like a field. It initially represented a place to reside that could provide food, as opposed to the outside world, which was considered dangerous and unpredictable.

Evolution of pictographic characters:

Traditional Chinese Wedding

chuán

传

tǒng

统

hūn

婚

sú

俗

As in most countries, weddings in China are joyous occasions, where two families come together in a celebration involving many important traditions (and staggering amounts of food). The traditional Chinese wedding dates back thousands of years. However, because of the recent Western influence, many young Chinese couples try and incorporate certain Western elements in their weddings. A wedding in China, traditional or otherwise, invariably follows ten very specific customs.

1. Gift giving
If you attend a wedding in China, you have to bring a gift for the happy couple. In the current day and age, this gift is usually what is referred to as a 'red envelope', which simply contains money.

2. Collecting the bride
On the morning of the wedding, the groom, his best man and the groomsmen have to pick up the bride from her home and escort her to where the wedding is to take place.

3. The tea offering
When collecting the bride, the groom has to make an offering of tea, fresh fruit and flowers to his future in-laws, as a sign of gratitude for the hand of their daughter.

4. Leaving home
After the tea offering, the bride leaves her family home along with her bridesmaids, who march behind her, holding decorative red umbrellas and throwing rice. They escort the bride to a ceremonial litter, which will take her to her new home.

5. The new home
This was traditionally the first time the bride entered the home she would be living in with her future husband. Nowadays it is more of a symbolic gesture, as couples often move in together before marriage. The bride then meets her future in-laws, provides a tea and fresh fruit offering, and they then all pray for their happiness and to their ancestors.

What does a traditional Chinese wedding look like? Is it similar to a Western wedding? Let's find out!

6. The banquet seating

This is a very important step, as seating arrangements aren't chosen at random at a Chinese wedding. Family and friends have to wait to be seated by the host, who will seat them in accordance with a specific hierarchy. Sitting in the wrong place is a terrible faux pas.

7. The toast to all guests

The couple are required to go around the banquet area and drink a toast with each guest or small group of guests, to thank them for their attendance and their gift. The drink in question is usually Chinese rice wine of the finest quality.

8. The bridal suite

After the ceremony, the bride and groom pray to heaven and earth, and pray for their parents. They then proceed to the bridal suite, escorted by the bridesmaids, groomsmen and many guests.

9. The hazing of couple

A popular wedding custom, while everyone is in the bridal suite, is to tease and play pranks on the couple - much like a hazing ritual. This is to make the situation less awkward for the bride and groom, who traditionally may have just met on their wedding day.

10. The return

The newlyweds have to visit the bride's parents exactly three days after the wedding ceremony. They must bring gifts, such as chickens, fresh fruit, tea and cakes. It is important to note that now that she is married, the bride is greeted by her parents not as their daughter, but as a guest.

huó

活

dòng

动

Activities

The subject of this chapter is actions and activities. We'll begin with a list of vocabulary focusing on leisure and athletic pastimes. We'll then move on to tackle three different ways to say 'can/could'. These are deceptively important in the Chinese language. From leisure activities we'll then progress to daily routine tasks such as 'going to work' or 'taking a shower'. We will also cover two additional grammar points: the present continuous and the past tense. This lesson will help you converse about hobbies and routine occupations.

dǎ
打

打 is a verb associated with actions that use the hands. It doesn't have a direct English equivalent and the translation depends on the action. For instance, here 打电话 is 'to make a phone call' and 打篮球 is 'to play basketball'.

diàn huà
电 话

lán qiú
篮 球

kàn
看

看 is a word used when mentioning actions that use the eyes. It could be 'look', 'see', 'watch', or even 'read' when talking about books. For example, 看电视 is 'to watch TV' or 看书 is 'to read a book'.

diàn shì
电 视

diàn yǐng
电 影

tīng
听

听 can mean 'to listen' or 'to hear'. The left part is the radical for 'mouth', and the right part originally looked like an ear. The initial meaning of the character was 'to lend an attentive ear when others are talking'. Now it can be used as in 听音乐, which is 'to listen to music'.

shū
书

yīn yuè
音 乐

can

会 is one of the Chinese characters meaning 'can'. However it is employed slightly differently to 能 or 可以. 会 is strictly employed as in 'to have the ability/knowledge to do something'. For example, 我会打篮球 is 'I can play basketball' as in 'I know how to play basketball'.
e.g. 会打篮球、会看

can

可以 is different from 'hui' (see above), as it is best translated by 'may' or 'be allowed to'. It is used to convey having another person's permission. Similarly 不可以 means that permission has not been granted. For instance, 你不可以看电视 is 'you can't watch TV' as in 'you're not allowed to watch TV'.
e.g. 可以看书、可以看电视

can

能 falls somewhere in between 会 and 可以. It can be used to describe 'be able to' as well as 'having permission'. It can also be used to convey possibility. For example, 你能来我家吗? means 'could you come to my house?' as in 'is it possible for you to come to my house?'
e.g. 能喝水、能看电影、能去

Action in progress

We've come across 在 in a previous chapter (see page 79), here however it has a slightly different use: it is used to describe actions in progress, similar to the English present continuous tense. For example, 我在吃米饭 means 'I'm (currently) eating rice'.

e.g. 在听音乐、在吃米饭

shuì jiào
睡觉

sleep

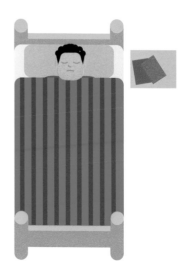

睡觉 means either 'to sleep' or 'to fall asleep'. 睡觉 is considered the verb part of the phrase. 睡 is a verb part which means 'to close the eyes' or 'to rest', and 觉 is a noun denoting a period of time during which a person is at rest. For instance 他在睡觉 is 'he is sleeping'.

e.g. 几点睡觉、能睡觉

qǐ chuáng
起床

get up

起床 means to 'to get up' or 'to wake up'. Like 睡觉 it is also a verb part of the phrase. 床 is 'bed' whereas 起 means 'to rise' or 'to sit up'. Therefore, the two together mean 'to get out of bed', hence 'to get up'.

e.g. 什么时候起床、爸爸起床

xǐ zǎo
洗澡

shower

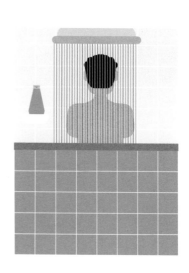

洗澡 literally means 'to wash oneself', although nowadays it mostly implies taking a shower or a bath. 洗 is the verbal part meaning 'to clean' or 'to wash', and 澡 has a similar meaning, although it is the word that relates to a noun.

e.g. 去洗澡、下午洗澡

to do

米做 is a general and adaptable verb. Depending on the action, it can either mean 'to do (something)', or 'to make (something)'. It means 'to make' when the action involves hands, for instance 我在做饭 is 'I'm making food'. When it refers to an activity or an event that is more abstract, it usually means 'to do'. For instance 你在做什么 is 'what are you doing?'

e.g. 做什么、做米饭、不喜欢做

work

The character 班 is mostly used to describe small work or study organizations. However it is more commonly used in conjunction with 上 (up) and 下 (down) to form 上班, which means 'to go to work' and 下班, which is 'to leave work'. It can also mean 'class' as in a class of students.

e.g. 上班、下班、我的班

class

课 can be translated as 'lesson' or 'class'. Just like 班 above, it can be paired with 上 and 下 to make 'to go to class' or 'to leave class'. This word can be employed by both teachers and students. If a teacher says 我在上课 it means 'I'm having class', with the implication that he/she is teaching the class.

e.g. 上课、下课

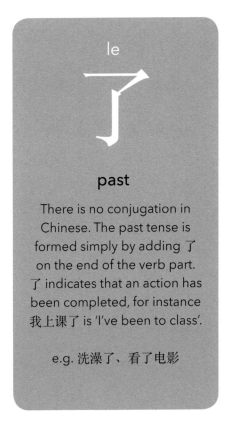

past

There is no conjugation in Chinese. The past tense is formed simply by adding 了 on the end of the verb part. 了 indicates that an action has been completed, for instance 我上课了 is 'I've been to class'.

e.g. 洗澡了、看了电影

Exploring the Language

Let's have a look at how to talk about the stage that an action has reached. As we have seen in earlier chapters, we usually use time words to indicate when an action happens instead of conjugating the verb. However, we also use modifiers to specify the stage of an action. For example, 在 is added to indicate that an action is ongoing. It goes immediately before the verb. 了 is another essential modifier. It signifies that the action has ended, so it is often used when talking about past events.

Person	-ing	action

Someone is in the progress of doing something.

Person	action	ended

Someone did or has done something.

For example:

   。

I am taking a shower.

  。

I took a shower.

   。

You didn't take a shower.

lóng long nǐ zài zuò shén me
龙龙,你在做什么?

wǒ zài shuì jiào nǐ ne
我在睡觉,你呢?

duì bù qǐ wǒ zài kàn shū
对不起!我在看书。

méi guān xi nǐ zěn me yàng
没关系,你怎么样?

Longlong & Xiongmao in China

wǒ hěn hǎo nǐ huì dǎ lán qiú ma
我很好,你会打篮球吗?

wǒ huì dǎ lán qiú wǒ zuó tiān dǎ lán qiú le
我会打篮球,我昨天打篮球了。

nǐ xià wǔ néng hé wǒ men dǎ lán qiú ma
你下午能和我们打篮球吗?

hǎo xià wǔ jiàn
好,下午见!

Practice Time

Now we're going to look at Xiongmao's daily planner. Using what we have learned in this chapter as a guide, try and match his activities with the appropriate time.

Hopefully now you're able to talk about activities as well as stating the time and place these activities will happen!

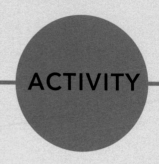

èr líng yī qī	nián	liù	yuè	sān	rì
二零一七	年	六	月	三	日

1. jiǔ diǎn qǐ chuáng
   九 点 起床 。

2. jiǔ diǎn sān shí fēn xǐ zǎo
   九 点 三十 分 洗澡

3. shí diǎn sì shí fēn kàn shū
   十 点 四十 分 看书

4. sān diǎn èr shí fēn dǎ lán qiú
   三 点 二十 分 打篮球

5. shí yī diǎn shuì jiào
   十一 点 睡觉 。

Basic Characters

to look

In early versions of this pictogram there is a clearly identifiable eye (bottom right). Above it there is supposed to be a hand shielding the eye from sunlight to help the observer see into the distance. Over the years it has evolved to become more consistent with other characters.

Evolution of pictographic characters:

to listen

When observing the earliest form of this character one can recognize an ear with two mouths on either side. It symbolized being attentive to one's entourage. Over time one of the two mouths was taken out and the design of the ear changed considerably.

Evolution of pictographic characters:

Traditional Chinese Medicines

zhōng
中

guó
国

zhōng
中

yī
医

Chinese medicine refers to the traditional use of herbal remedies and other healing methods invented in China by the Han people. Its origin can be traced back to the Shang dynasty (14th–11th centuries BCE). However at that time, ailments were not viewed as diseases but instead as curses from the ancestral gods. China was one of the first countries in the world to have a medical culture, and its approach to healing differs substantially from Western medicine. It has heavily influenced the healing methods of other Asian countries; Japanese and Korean medicines are both based on Chinese medicine.

Chinese medicine is unique due to its naturalistic and philosophical roots. Ancient Chinese healers theorized that humans, just like any other aspect of the natural world, are comprised of Yin and Yang, two contrary yet complementary forces. In a healthy human being, the Yin and Yang would be in a state of equality and balance. However, when they are in imbalance or inequality, symptoms start to appear. Chinese medicine strives to redress that balance to cure the sufferer from their afflictions.

One of the core elements of Chinese medicine is what Chinese doctors call 恒动观 (héng dòng guān), which can be translated as 'ever-changing outlook'. This refers to the belief that humans are part of nature, and that disease is brought on by changes in nature, such as climate, environment or temperature. Chinese medical practitioners would consider the time (of year, season, or even day), the environment, and the individual in question to inform their diagnosis. There are four traditional methods of Chinese diagnosis, known as observation, auscultation, interrogation and the taking of the pulse and palpation.

Observation

Known as 望 (wang), the observation stage of Chinese diagnosis involves taking an overview of the patient's appearance and making a note of any abnormalities. Chinese medicine operates according to the principle that different facial features are intrinsically linked with specific internal organs. For example, the eyes are linked with the liver, the tongue with the heart, and the nose with the lungs. Therefore, abnormal coloration of the tongue would be symptomatic of heart problems.

Chinese medicine has a unique and philosophical way of looking at illness. What is it all about?

Auscultation

This stage is called 闻 (wen) in Chinese. It involves listening to sounds emitted from the patient's body, such as heavy breathing, stomach rumbles, heart rate, coughing etc. It also involves the olfactory sense, as Chinese doctors inform their diagnosis with possible abnormal smells emanating from the patient. This helps the practitioner gain extra information on what the patient might be suffering from and how to cure it.

Interrogation

Referred to as 问 (wen), this step involves asking the patient and his or her relatives a series of medical questions. In order to fully evaluate the situation, a Chinese doctor will invariably ask: when the symptoms first manifested themselves, what the patient thinks might have brought on the affliction, the evolution of the symptoms, and family medical history. Doctors might also ask whether the patient is in any pain, what sort of lifestyle they lead and about their eating habits.

Pulse and palpation

This is called 切 (qie). It simply involves taking a patient's pulse by tapping two fingers on the radial artery to note any changes in heartbeat. This informs the doctor about the state of the patient's internal energies. From very early on, the Chinese determined the correlation between heartbeat and blood circulation, and established that an irregular pulse was a sign that specific internal organs weren't receiving a sufficient flow of internal energy.

miáo

描

shù

述

Describing Things

This chapter is all about descriptions. We'll start by learning to discuss weather conditions and how to explain temperatures. We'll also cover basic descriptive adjectives and adverbs, such as 'big' and 'small', 'fast' and 'slow'. We will move on to introduce two important character modifiers. The first is useful for connecting an adjective with a noun, while the second is used to describe the action of a verb. This lesson will include new and practical grammar points, which will be helpful in constructing more complex sentences.

Building Blocks

big

大, when describing objects, is an adjective meaning 'big'. However when talking about people, the meaning changes to 'old'.
e.g. 大苹果、大飞机

small

小 in Chinese means 'small' or 'little'. However the meaning changes to 'young' when it is used to describe people.
e.g. 小苹果、小饭馆

many

多 has the meaning of 'more' or 'many'. It is commonly paired with 很 to form 很多, which means 'many', as in 'a lot'.
e.g. 很多、不多

few

少 means 'few', 'little' or 'less'. It is a modification of the character 小 and is used to describe a small quantity.
e.g. 很少、不少

fast

快 means 'fast', 'quick', or 'quickly'. It can be used to describe objects and people as well as actions. For instance, 他很快 means 'he's very fast'.
e.g. 太快、不很快

slow

慢 is the Chinese word for 'slow' or 'slowly'. In a similar way to 快 (left) it applies to objects and people, as well as actions.
e.g. 不慢、太慢

description

The character 的 is a very useful one, with several important uses. On top of turning pronouns into possessive pronouns, it is used to connect descriptive phrases with nouns. For example, 漂亮的小姐 means 'a pretty woman'.

e.g. 他的、漂亮的、很小的

adverb

The character 得 is defined as a 'descriptive complement'. It is used to describe the action of a verb. We usually state the action, followed by 得, and then by a descriptive word. For instance, 我说得快 means 'I speak fast'. An example of a negative would be 我开得不快 'I don't drive fast'.

e.g. 做得快、吃得少

piào   liang

漂亮

beautiful

漂亮 is used to describe something 'beautiful', 'pretty' or 'good-looking'. It is more commonly used to describe women, but can also be applied to things in nature, works of art or particular objects.

e.g. 很漂亮、不漂亮

to rain

下 means 'down' and 雨 is the character for 'rain'. Therefore 下雨 can be translated as 'it's raining'. For instance, 今天下雨 would be 'it's raining today'.

e.g. 今天下雨、不下雨

to snow

雪 is the character for snow. Just like 雨 it can be paired with 下 to form 下雪 meaning 'it's snowing'. For example, 昨天下雪了 is 'it was snowing yesterday'.

e.g. 下大雪、明天下雪

cold

The character 冷 means 'cold'. The radical 冫 on the left means 'ice', which is similar to the water radical 氵, but with one less stroke. 今天很冷 means 'it's very cold today'.

e.g. 不冷、太冷了

hot

热 is used to describe something hot. The bottom part of the character represents a cooking pit and resembles flames. 米饭太热 would be 'the rice is too hot!'

e.g. 很热、不太热

sunny

晴 means 'sunny'. On the left there is the radical for 'sun', and the 青 on the right-hand side is there to indicate pronunciation. 今天是晴天 means 'today is a sunny day'.

e.g. 今天晴、晴天

cloudy

阴 is the character for 'cloudy'. On the right of the character there is the radical 月, which means 'moon', which is evocative of a cloudy night sky. 天很阴 means 'the sky is very cloudy'.

e.g. 昨天阴、阴天

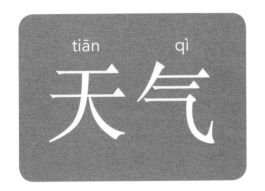

weather

天 can mean either 'sky' or 'day', and 气 is the character for 'air'. 天气 come together to mean 'weather'. The expression is supposed to be representative of the changes in the sky and in the air. 天气很好 would mean 'the weather is lovely'.

e.g. 天气怎么样、天气不好

temperature

温(wēn)度(dù) together mean 'temperature'. For instance, 今天多少度 means 'what is the temperature today?'. However 度 on its own means 'degrees' (Celsius unless otherwise specified). For example, a possible answer to the previous question could be 今天三十二度 which means 'it is 32 degrees today'.

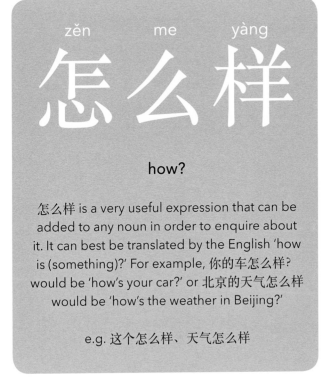

how?

怎么样 is a very useful expression that can be added to any noun in order to enquire about it. It can best be translated by the English 'how is (something)?' For example, 你的车怎么样? would be 'how's your car?' or 北京的天气怎么样 would be 'how's the weather in Beijing?'

e.g. 这个怎么样、天气怎么样

Exploring the Language

Let have a look at how to describe an object or an action in Chinese. There are two 'de' commonly used in Chinese. Despite being different characters, they both have the same pronunciation. The first 'de' 的 is used to describe a noun. It connects the description with the noun, and the phrase comes immediately before the noun. The second 'de' 得 is used to describe a verb. It connects the description with the verb, and the phrase comes right after the verb instead. Knowing how to employ these two 'de' appropriately will enrich your sentences and add more flavour and colour to your daily communications in Chinese.

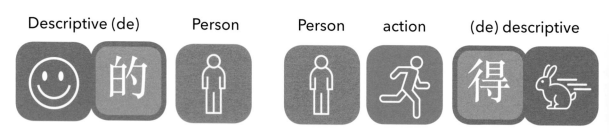

Describing a person or an object.   Describing how well an action is performed.

For example:

Pretty woman.

I drive very well.

Do you drive well?

lóng long nǐ hǎo nǐ zěn me yàng
龙龙,你好!你怎么样?

wǒ hěn hǎo nǐ ne
我很好,你呢?

wǒ yě hěn hǎo xiè xie
我也很好,谢谢!

jīn tiān tiān qì zěn me yàng
今天天气怎么样?

Longlong & Xiongmao in China

jīn tiān xià yǔ xià de hěn dà
今天下雨,下得很大。

jīn tiān lěng ma
今天冷吗?

bù lěng èr shí wǔ dù nǐ nà er lěng ma
不冷,二十五度。你那儿冷吗!

bù lěng wǒ zhè er èr shí sān dù
不冷,我这儿二十三度。

Practice Time

Using what we have learned in this chapter as a guide, read the following sentences and decide which picture best describes the sentence.

Remember, if a descriptive word is an adjective it comes before the noun, and if it is an adverb it comes after the verb.

1
hěn duō
很 多
píng guǒ
苹 果
 ☐   ☐

2
jīn tiān
今 天
xià yǔ
下 雨
 ☐   ☐

3
chē
车
kāi
开
de
得
kuài
快
 ☐   ☐

4
tā
他
bù
不
lěng
冷
 ☐   ☐

5
jīn tiān
今 天
èr shí
二 十
dù
度
 ☐   ☐

Basic Characters

big

The earlier versions of this character originally represented an adult male with open arms and legs parted, standing in a towering position of power and dominance. Initially it meant 'an adult'. The meaning has changed over time, yet the character has changed relatively little.

Evolution of pictographic characters:

---

small

The three lines present in the early form of this character were meant to represent three grains of sand. This was also the character's first meaning before it changed to 'little' or 'small'. When 小's meaning changed, scholars created a new character for 'sand' by adding the water radical 氵 to 小 to create 沙 (sha).

Evolution of pictographic characters:

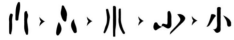

Chinese Idioms: Chengyu

zhōng
中

guó
国

chéng
成

yǔ
语

成语 (chéng yǔ) are idioms that have been gathered over thousands of years of Chinese history. They form a unique part of Chinese language. Similar to some English proverbs, they have a set structure and pre-set meaning, and are used as an entity when constructing sentences. Most Chengyu come from ancient Chinese tales. They are usually grammatically different to modern Chinese and are used in a different way to more recent phrases and sayings. They are shining examples of the poetic possibilities of the Chinese language that have enriched conversations for centuries.

Chengyu tend to be short, usually consisting of four characters. They can be as short as three characters, and some of them have as many as eight, although these are very rare. They have their roots either in Chinese classical works of literature, East Asian history or folk tales. Most Chinese people would have heard or studied these stories from an early age, and would use Chengyu to summarize them to make a point in conversation. Much like Western maxims and proverbs, Chengyu often deal with morality, and try to teach edifying life lessons through storytelling.

Characteristics of Chengyu

Set structure – The structure of a Chengyu cannot be modified and its components cannot be replaced. If the Chengyu's component characters are altered, the meaning behind the original metaphor is lost.

Meaning – Simply understanding and knowing the character does not give people the true meaning of a Chengyu. One has to read between the lines to really understand its intentions. It also helps to know the story behind the saying.

Flexible grammar – If we look at a Chengyu's grammatical structure, its use could be quite flexible. They are removed from modern Chinese grammar and can affect a sentence differently, depending on whether they're added to nouns or verbs.

Stylistic touch – Appropriately using Chengyu in conversation will help any Chinese speaker to have a more expressive and colourful use of the language. Furthermore, they are useful tools to help make a point in a concise manner.

刻舟求剑

to mark the boat where the sword fell off

Many years ago, a man from the state of Chu went on a voyage. While his boat was crossing the river, he drew his sword to cut a piece of rope. Suddenly, a wave crashed into the ship and caused him to lose his balance, whereupon he accidentally dropped his sword into the depths of the river. His fellow voyagers cried out 'Your sword just fell off the boat!' Despite everyone's alarm, the man was not at all worried. He quickly marked the boat with a sharp knife at the place where the sword fell and calmly said, 'Don't worry. I have everything under control.' His comrades were confused by his behaviour, and kept pressing him to dive into the water before it was too late. He remained calm and explained: 'Why are you so worried? I have marked the boat where I lost the sword.' Once they had reached the other side of the river, the man announced, 'Now I will dive into the river from the mark I made on the boat. I'll be sure to find my sword!' He swam and swam, but his sword was nowhere to be found. He went back to the shore completely bewildered, with his companions laughing at him behind his back. This idiom tells us that we live in an ever-changing world, and that our perspective must adapt to our surroundings and to each new situation. Legend has it that this story was first told to an emperor, to warn him against clinging to archaic traditions without considering the changes in the country.

狐假虎威

the fox exploits the tiger's might

Once upon a time, a fierce tiger was roaming through the forest, hunting for food. As he wandered into a clearing he saw a fox. As quick as a flash, he pounced and caught the fox in his mighty claws. The fox was terrified! But he was also clever and cunning. Before the tiger could eat him, he cried out, 'I was sent to the forest by the gods in the sky. They have appointed me to be the king of the forest! If you harm me, the gods are sure to come down and punish you severely for your crime!' The tiger was confused, unsure if he should believe the fox. So he said, 'You'll have to prove it!' The fox replied, 'Take a stroll with me around the forest. You'll see how I'm revered and feared by all the other animals.' After much thought, the tiger agreed this would be a reasonable way of finding out the truth. And so they went through the forest, with the fox in front and the tiger following behind. Rabbits, goats, deer and bears all fled in terror upon seeing the mighty tiger and his companion. 'Do you believe me now?' the fox asked the tiger. 'Did you see a single animal who wasn't scared of me? That's because I am king of the forest!' The tiger didn't realize that all the animals were, in fact, scared of him. Not only did the fox escape being eaten, but all the other animals thought he had tamed the ferocious tiger. This idiom can tell us an agile mind can be mightier than brute force. It also tells us that things aren't always what they seem, and that there are some who will manipulate the powerful to gain power for themselves.

shēng

huó

大家好！

Work and Study

In this final chapter, we'll look at the subjects of studying and jobs. We'll begin by introducing some new vocabulary related to these topics that will include various job titles and words that can be used in a professional or classroom environment. We'll move on to words specifically about learning Chinese. These words are essential to anyone wishing to have an in-depth understanding of the Chinese language. This chapter will be helpful for communicating with other members of a student body or professional environment. It will also introduce new elements of Chinese culture.

Building Blocks

teacher
老师 is the word for 'teacher'. 老 means 'old' or 'senior' and 师 means 'master', referring to someone professional who has a lot of knowledge to pass on.
e.g. 是老师、好老师

xué	shēng

student
学生 is the word for 'student'. The first character 学 means 'to study' or 'to learn', and 生 means 'birth' or 'life', but here has extended its meaning to 'person'. A 学生 is therefore a person who studies.
e.g. 他的学生、学生上课

tóng	xué

classmate
同学 is similar to the English word 'classmate'. 同 means 'the same' and 学 means 'to study'. 同学 therefore designates people from the same study group.
e.g. 他的同学、我们的同学

friend
朋友 means 'friend'. The character 朋 originally looked like two bracelets tied together, symbolizing like-minded people helping each other in need.
e.g. 好朋友、朋友的狗

yī	shēng

doctor
医生 means 'doctor'. 医 used to mean 'to look after the wounded' and can be found in most expressions relating to medical professions.
e.g. 我的一生、很多一生

painter
画家 is 'painter'. The character 画 means 'to paint' or 'to sketch' or 'to draw', whereas 家 denotes someone who is accomplished in their field. 家 can be added to other words, such as 音乐家 meaning 'musician'.
e.g. 画家的画、没有画家

Working or studying in China? Let's find out how to say we're doing that.

gōng zuò
工作

to work

工作 can either be a noun for 'job' or a verb meaning 'to work'. The character 工 was first modelled on an ancient tool commonly used by craftsmen. Similarly, 作 was initially meant to look like a carpenter's workstation. 你在哪儿工作 would be 'where do you work?' (verb) and 我喜欢我的工作 would be 'I like my job'.
e.g. 朋友的工作、工作是 什么

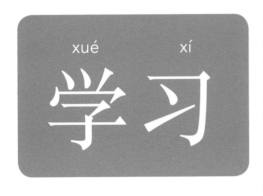

xué xí
学习

to study

学习 is a verb meaning 'to study'. It can be shortened to 学, but 学 by itself and 学习 have very different implications. 学 is used when the study is more casual or leisurely, whereas 学习 implies more dedication and effort. For example, 我喜欢学汉语 means 'I like learning Chinese (for fun/as a hobby)' whereas 我去中国学习汉语 means 'I'm going to China to study Chinese.'
e.g. 爱学习、学生学习

listen

听 is for activities that require ears, similar to 'to hear' or 'to listen to (something)' in English.
e.g. 听音乐、听你

speak

The character 说 means 'to speak' or 'to say'. It can be used either as 'to say something', 'to speak to someone', or as in 'to speak a language'.
e.g. 说汉语、不说

read

读 means 'to read'. We've previously learnt the expression 看书 for 'to read a book' (see page 90). However 读书 is slightly more formal.
e.g. 读书、读汉语

write

写 means 'to write'. It can be used for specific writing, such as 写字 'to write characters' or more generally, such as 写书 'to write a book'.
e.g. 写汉字、喜欢写

běi jīng
北京

Beijing

北京 is the capital of China. It literally means 'north capital'. It is the most recent and most successful capital city in Chinese history. There is also 南京 (najing), which is 'south capital' and 东京 (donjing), which is the Chinese word for 'Tokyo', and literally means 'east capital'.

e.g. 中国北京、在北京

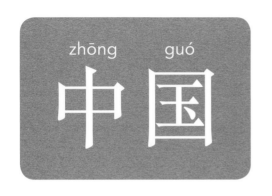

China

中国 is the word the Chinese use when referring to their country. The character 中 refers to 'middle' and to the central plain of Asia, also known as the Yellow River region, where the Chinese civilization first flourished. China has over 5,000 years of history, from small native tribes to the only survivors of four great ancient civilizations.

e.g. 中国饭店、在中国

Chinese

汉语 is the Chinese word for their own language. 汉 (or Han in English) is the largest ethnicity in China, comprising 91.51 per cent of the country's population. The character 语 means 'language'. Therefore 汉语 literally means 'the language of the Han'.

e.g. 说汉语、读汉语

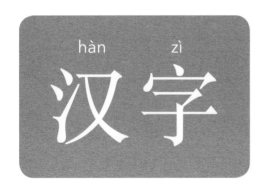

Characters

汉字 is the word for 'Chinese characters'. The character 字 simply means 'character' or 'ideogram'. It originally began as a symbol to mark on a baby's head to indicate who it belonged to and to prevent anyone else from stealing it. This is why we can find this character in 名字 (name). The expression 汉字 literally means 'the Han's characters'.

e.g. 写汉字、中国的汉字

Exploring the Language

In this final chapter let's have a quick review of how to learn Chinese. We hope by now you have a better understanding of the 'Chinese way' of thinking. It is simple, clear and logical, and constructing Chinese sentences is like putting together puzzle pieces. Chinese is different to English in that it can be likened to building blocks. As long as we understand the main structure, the blocks are easily interchangeable. Hopefully this book has given you the right tools to continue exploring the world of the Chinese language.

Person	Time	Place	Action
Sentences always start with the subject. It can be a person, several people or an object. It is most commonly a noun.	The part of a sentence referring to time appears immediately after the person. They are used more frequently than in English because of the lack of conjugation in Chinese.	The phrase that helps to indicate the location of something needs to come after the word relating to time, but before the action.	Unlike many Western languages, the action usually appears at the end of a sentence. There can be one or more actions.

For example:

  o

I'm going to study Chinese in China next year.

  ?

What are you going to study in China next year?

lóng long nǐ hǎo nǐ rèn shi tiān tiān ma
龙龙你好。你认识天天吗？

wǒ rèn shi tiān tiān tā shì wǒ de péng yǒu
我认识天天。他是我的朋友。

tiān tiān zuò shén me
天天做什么？

tiān tiān zài zhōng guó xué hàn yǔ
天天在中国学汉语。

Longlong & Xiongmao in China

tā shuō hàn yǔ shuō de hěn hǎo ma
他说汉语说得很好吗？

shì tā xiǎng qù běi jīng zuò lǎo shī
是，他想去北京做老师。

tā xiě hàn zì xiě de hǎo ma
他写汉字写得好吗？

tā xiě hàn zì xiě de hěn hǎo
他写汉字写得很好。

Practice Time

Using what we have learned in this chapter as a guide, try to put the right vocabulary cards into the correct sentence. The colour will help you determine what the function of the word is.

When turning a sentence into a question, keep the structure and replace the element in question with the question word.

A.
shuí
谁

B.
nǎ er
哪儿

C.
shén me
什么

D.
shén me shí hòu
什么时候

1.
wǒ
我
jīn tiān
今天
zài
在
[ ]
mǎi
买
niú nǎi
牛奶
?

2.
nǐ
你
[ ]
zài
在
xué xiào
学校
xué
学
hàn yǔ
汉语
?

3.
tā
她
zuó tiān
昨天
zài
在
yī yuàn
医院
zuò
做
[ ]
?

4.
[ ]
míng tiān
明天
zài
在
fàn guǎn
饭馆
chī
吃
wǔ fàn
午饭
?

Basic Characters

middle

On observing the early form of 中 we can notice two flags opposing each other, with a circle in between them. The flags were meant to represent warring armies, while the circle represented a no-fight zone, separating the enemy factions.

Evolution of pictographic characters:

country

In the current version of this character we can identify the radical 口, meaning 'border' and 'city walls', and between these walls is 王, which is the character for 'king' or 'military leader'. The notion being that a country requires a ruler to protect its borders.

Evolution of pictographic characters:

The Four Great Chinese Innovations

sì
四

dà
大

chuàng
创

xīn
新

Historically, China has been known for its technological advancements and innovations in fields such as mechanics, hydraulics and mathematics. Four inventions stand out in China's history and are known as 'The Four Great Chinese Inventions'. These are the compass, gunpowder, woodblock printing and paper. Technology still has a very important place in Chinese society and in the day-to-day life of Chinese citizens. It is also possible to identify several recent innovations that have had a great influence on everyday life in China.

Compass

Gunpowder

Woodblock printing

Paper

高速铁路
High Speed Rail (HSR)

High-velocity trains have been in operation in many other countries including Japan and France. However, the Chinese have implemented them on a large scale and have managed to make travelling on them affordable for the majority of its citizens. The Chinese HSR network currently runs for 22,000km, and operated 2,595 trains in 2016, which makes up 60 per cent of the world's high-speed journeys. HSR trains in China run at speeds ranging from 250km/h to 350km/h. Engineers are currently working on the next generation of bullet train, which is set to reach speeds of up to 400km/h.

You must have heard of the great four Chinese inventions. What about the great four innovations?

共享单车
The dockless bicycle

Although the concept of shared bikes originated in Europe, the Chinese took it a step further by eliminating the need for docking stations. These bikes can be found all around major cities in China, and combine GPS technology, smartphone apps and mobile payments. One can easily use one's phone to find the nearest bike and book it. They're unlocked simply by scanning a code generated by a mobile app. Once the journey is over, the rider physically locks the bike and the appropriate fare will be debited from his/her account. It has significantly reduced traffic and the carbon imprint of most Chinese cities.

移动支付
mobile payment

China nowadays is almost a 'cashless' society. There are two companies, Alipay and Tenpay, which act as third-party platforms to allow people to pay securely for almost any commodity or service in China using mobile phones. To pay for a product or service, the buyer's app generates a QR code, which the seller scans using their phone. This has eliminated the need for cash or card machines and has greatly streamlined the payment process in many commercial outlets in China. Mobile payments also permit money transfers between individuals by way of text messaging. These money transfer texts are often referred to as Hong Bao (red packet), the same name given to the money-filled envelopes commonly offered as wedding gifts.

网上购物
E-commerce

China is the largest and fastest-growing e-commerce market. Websites such as TaoBao and JD.com have decentralized the Chinese online shopping system, and have allowed small retailers to have an online space from which to sell their products and reach a very wide audience. One of the reasons for the recent e-commerce boom is the efficiency of product delivery, even for cross-country distances, and product tracking. E-commerce has also been very beneficial to rural areas of the country, allowing them to trade more easily with coastal cities and improve their quality of life. The rise of e-commerce has created over 20 million new jobs in Chinese rural areas in 2016.

Glossary

English - Chinese

apple	苹果	píngguǒ
auxiliary for adverb	得	dé
auxiliary for past action	了	le
auxiliary for possession and adjective	的	de
basketball	篮球	lánqiú
be	是	shì
beautiful	漂亮	piàoliang
before	前	qián
behind	后	hòu
Beijing	北京	běijīng
big	大	dà
book	书	shū
bus	公交车	gōngjiāo chē
buy	买	mǎi
call	叫	jiào
can (ability and permission)	能	néng
can (ability)	会	huì
can (permission)	可以	kěyǐ
cat	猫	māo
chair	椅子	yǐzi
cheap	便宜	piányí
China	中国	zhōngguó
Chinese	汉语	hànyǔ
Chinese character	汉字	hànzì
class	班	bān
classmate	同学	tóngxué
clothes	衣服	yīfú
cloudy	阴	yīn
coffee	咖啡	kāfēi
cold	冷	lěng
computer	电脑	diànnǎo
cup	杯子	bēizi
daughter	女儿	nǚ'ér
day	日	rì
day	天	tiān
do	做	zuò

doctor	医生	yīshēng
dog	狗	gǒu
drink	喝	hē
drive	开	kāi
eat	吃	chī
egg	鸡蛋	jīdàn
eight	八	bā
expensive	贵	guì
family	家	jiā
fast	快	kuài
father	爸爸	bàba
few	少	shǎo
first name	名字	míngzi
five	五	wǔ
four	四	sì
friend	朋友	péngyǒu
general measure word	个	gè
get up	起床	qǐchuáng
go to bed	睡觉	shuìjiào
good	好	hǎo
goodbye	再见	zàijiàn
happy	高兴	gāoxìng
have, there is	有	yǒu
he	他	tā
hello	你好	nǐ hǎo
hello (on phone)	喂	wèi
here	这儿	zhè'er
hospital	医院	yīyuàn
hot	热	rè
how	怎么	zěnme
how about	呢	ne
how is	怎么样	zěnme yàng
how many	多少	duōshǎo
how many	几	jǐ
I	我	wǒ
in	在	zài
in the afternoon	下午	xiàwǔ
inside	里	lǐ
it's OK	没关系	méiguānxì
left	左	zuǒ
lesson	课	kè

like	喜欢	xǐhuān
listen	听	tīng
live	住	zhù
look	看	kàn
love	爱	ài
many	多	duō
measure word for books	本	běn
milk	牛奶	niúnǎi
minute	分	fēn
Miss	小姐	xiǎojiě
moment	时候	shíhòu
money	钱	qián
month	月	yuè
morning	上午	shàngwǔ
mother	妈妈	māma
Mr	先生	xiānshēng
music	音乐	yīnyuè
nine	九	jiǔ
noon	午	wǔ
noon	中午	zhōngwǔ
not	不	bù
not (have)	没	méi
now	现在	xiànzài
o'clock	点	diǎn
on	上	shàng
one	一	yī
outside	外	wài
painter	画家	huàjiā
people	人	rén
phone	电话	diànhuà
plane	飞机	fēijī
please	请	qǐng
rain	下雨	xià yǔ
read	读	dú
restaurant	饭馆	fànguǎn
rice	米饭	mǐ fàn
right	右	yòu
school	学校	xuéxiào
sell	卖	mài
seven	七	qī
ship	船	chuán
shop	商店	shāngdiàn
side	边	biān
side	面	miàn
six	六	liù
slow	慢	màn
small	小	xiǎo
snow	下雪	xià xuě
some	些	xiē
son	儿子	érzi
sorry	对不起	duìbùqǐ
speak	说	shuō
student	学生	xuéshēng
study	学习	xuéxí
sunny	晴	qíng
table	桌子	zhuōzi
take (a transport)	坐	zuò
take a shower	洗澡	xǐ zǎo
taxi	出租车	chūzū chē
tea	茶	chá
teacher	老师	lǎoshī
temperature	温度	wēndù
ten	十	shí
thank you	谢谢	xièxiè
that	那	nà
the film	电影	diànyǐng
there	那儿	nà'er
they	他们	tāmen
thing	东西	dōngxī
think, want to do	想	xiǎng
this	这	zhè
three	三	sān
to come	来	lái
to go	去	qù
to return	回	huí
today	今天	jīntiān
tomorrow	明天	míngtiān
too	太	tài
train	火车	huǒchē
train station	火车站	huǒchē zhàn
TV	电视	diànshì
two	二	èr
under	下	xià
understanding	认识	rènshì
unit for Chinese currency	块	kuài
use hand to do	打	dǎ
vegetables, dish	菜	cài
very	很	hěn
water	水	shuǐ
we	我们	wǒmen
weather	天气	tiānqì
week	星期	xīngqí
what	什么	shénme
where	哪儿	nǎ'er
which	哪	nǎ
who	谁	shuí
work	工作	gōngzuò
write	写	xiě
year	年	nián
year old	岁	suì

Chinese - English

面	miàn	side
明天	míngtiān	tomorrow
名字	míngzì	first name
那	nà	that
哪	nǎ	which
那儿	nà'er	there
哪儿	nǎ'er	where
呢	ne	how about
能	néng	can (ability and permission)
你	nǐ	you
你好	nǐ hǎo	hello
年	nián	year
你们	nǐmen	you (plural)
牛奶	niúnǎi	milk
女儿	nǚ'ér	daughter
朋友	péngyǒu	friend
便宜	piányí	cheap
漂亮	piàoliang	beautiful
苹果	píngguǒ	apple
七	qī	seven
钱	qián	money
前	qián	before
起床	qǐchuáng	get up
晴	qíng	sunny
请	qǐng	please
去	qù	to go
热	rè	hot
人	rén	people
认识	rènshì	understanding
日	rì	day
三	sān	three
上	shàng	on
商店	shāngdiàn	shop
上午	shàngwǔ	morning
少	shǎo	few
谁	shéi	who
什么	shénme	what
十	shí	ten
是	shì	be
时候	shíhòu	moment
书	shū	book
水	shuǐ	water
睡觉	shuìjiào	go to bed
说	shuō	speak
四	sì	four
岁	suì	year old
他	tā	he
太	tài	too
他们	tāmen	they
天	tiān	day
天气	tiānqì	weather

听	tīng	listen
同学	tóngxué	classmate
外	wài	outside
喂	wèi	hello (on phone)
温度	wēndù	temperature
我	wǒ	I
我们	wǒmen	we
五	wǔ	five
午	wǔ	noon
洗澡	xǐ zǎo	take a shower
下	xià	under
下雪	xià xuě	snow
下雨	xià yǔ	rain
想	xiǎng	think, want to do
先生	xiānshēng	Mr
现在	xiànzài	now
小	xiǎo	small
小姐	xiǎojiě	Miss
下午	xiàwǔ	in the afternoon
写	xiě	write
些	xiē	some
谢谢	xièxiè	thank you
喜欢	xǐhuān	like
星期	xīngqí	week
学生	xuéshēng	student
学习	xuéxí	study
学校	xuéxiào	school
一	yī	one
衣服	yīfú	clothes
阴	yīn	cloudy
音乐	yīnyuè	music
医生	yīshēng	doctor
医院	yīyuàn	hospital
椅子	yǐzi	chair
右	yòu	right
有	yǒu	have, there is
月	yuè	month
在	zài	in
再见	zàijiàn	goodbye
怎么	zěnme	how
怎么样	zěnme yàng	how is
这	zhè	this
这儿	zhè'er	here
中国	zhōngguó	China
中午	zhōngwǔ	noon
住	zhù	live
桌子	zhuōzi	table
坐	zuò	take (a transport)
做	zuò	do
左	zuǒ	left
昨天	zuótiān	yesterday

PRACTICE TIME ANSWERS

Chapter 1: People
我们 – we
他 – he
有 – have
不 – not
儿子 – son

Chapter 2: Time
1. 八点
2. 星期四
3. 一九二四年
4. 昨天
5. 今天
6. 明天
7. 一月
8. 八月
9. 六点二十分
10. 上午
11. 现在
12. 几点
13. 时候
14. 九年

Chapter 3: Encounters
你叫什么 – 我叫天天
再见 – 再见
你好吗 – 我很好
对不起 – 没关系
你几岁 – 我八岁
谢谢 – 不客气

Chapter 4: Going Places
Q1:   Q2:
1. 他   1. 你
2. 昨天下午   2. 早上八点
3. 坐飞机   3. 怎么
4. 去中国   4. 来北京

Chapter 5: Shopping
1. egg
2. milk
3. apple
4. coffee

Chapter 6: At Home
1. true
2. false
3. false
4. true

Chapter 7: Activities
1. 09:00 – get up
2. 09:30 – take a shower
3. 10:40 – reading
4. 15:20 – play basketball
5. 23:00 – go to bed

Chapter 8: Descriptions
6. A
7. A
8. B
9. A
10. A

Chapter 9: Work & Study
1. B
2. D
3. C
4. A

LONGLONG AND XIONGMAO IN CHINA

P23
XM: Who is this?
LL: This is my father.
XM: Who is that?
LL: That is my mother.
XM: Does Mr Wang have a son?
LL: No. He has a daughter.
XM: Which one is his daughter?
LL: That's his daughter.

P35
XM: What day is it today?
LL: Today is June 3rd.
XM: Which day of the week is it tomorrow?
LL: Tomorrow is Friday.
XM: What time is it now?
LL: It's 3.40 in the afternoon.

P47
XM: Hello! What's your name?
LL: Hello, I'm called Longlong. And you?
XM: I'm called Xiongmao.
LL: How old are you?
XM: I'm nine years old. How old are you?
LL: I'm ten years old.
XM: Nice to meet you!
LL: Nice to meet you too!

P59
XM: Hello, Longlong! Where are you going today?
LL: Hello, Xiongmao! I'm going to the shop today.
XM: When are you going to the shop?
LL: I'm going to the shop this afternoon.
XM: How are you going to the shop this afternoon?
LL: I'm going by bus.
XM: Great! Can I come with you?
LL: Brilliant, see you!

P71
XM: Hello! What do you want to buy today?
LL: I want to buy some apples. And you?
XM: Some vegetables and eggs. Do you like apples?
LL: I really like apples. And you?
XM: I like apples too!
LL: How much is it for apples?
XM: An apple costs one yuan, very cheap!
LL: Great! I'll buy five apples.

P83
XM: Longlong, do you have cats?
LL: Yes, I have a kitten and a puppy.
XM: Where is the puppy?
LL: The puppy is behind the TV.
XM: Where is the kitten?
LL: The kitten is under the chair.
XM: Does the kitten like the puppy?
LL: Yes! They both live under the table.

P95
XM: Hello! What are you doing?
LL: I was sleeping. And you?
XM: Sorry! I'm reading.
LL: It's OK. How are you?
XM: I'm very well. Can you play basketball?
LL: Yes, I can. I played yesterday.
XM: Can you play with us in the afternoon?
LL: Yes, see you in the afternoon!

P107
XM: Hello, Longlong! How are you?
LL: I'm very well, and you?
XM: I'm very well as well. Thanks!
LL: What's the weather like today?
XM: It is raining today, very heavily.
LL: Is it cold today?
XM: Not cold, 25 degrees. Is it cold at your place?
LL: Not cold, here it is 23 degrees.

P119
XM: Hello, Longlong. Do you know Tiantian?
LL: I know Tiantian. He is my friend.
XM: What does Tiantian do?
LL: Tiantian studies Chinese in China.
XM: He speaks Chinese very well.
LL: Yes, he wants to go to Beijing to be a teacher.
XM: Does he write Chinese characters well?
LL: Yes, he writes characters very well.

PROPERTY OF
LANIER ELEMENTARY